"I'll bet it's one of the big grizzlies we've heard about,"
said Teague.

That was something to my taste. I have seen a few
grizzlies. Riding to higher ground I kept close watch on
the few open patches up on the slope. The chase led
toward us for a while. Suddenly I saw a big bear with a
frosted coat go lumbering across one of these openings.

"Silvertip! Silvertip!" I yelled at the top of my lungs.
"I saw him!"

My call thrilled everybody. Vern spurred his horse and
took to the right. Teague advised that we climb the slope.
So we made for the timber. Once there we had to get off
and climb on foot. It was steep, rough, very hard work. I
had on chaps and spurs. Soon I was hot, laboring, and my
heart began to hurt. We all had to rest. The baying of the
hounds inspirited us . . .

ZANE GREY · Volume I
TALES OF LONELY TRAILS
FOREWORD BY LOREN GREY

CHARTER BOOKS, NEW YORK

FRONTISPIECE. Zane Grey

This Charter book contains the complete
text of the first half of the original edition.
It has been completely reset in a typeface
designed for easy reading and was printed
from new film.

TALES OF LONELY TRAILS
VOLUME 1

A Charter Book / published by arrangement with
Northland Press

PRINTING HISTORY
Harper and Brothers edition published 1922
Northland Press edition published 1986
Charter edition / February 1988

ISBN: 1-55773-004-0

Charter Books are published by The Berkley Publishing Group,
200 Madison Avenue, New York, New York 10016.
The name "CHARTER" and the "C" logo
are trademarks belonging to Charter Communications, Inc.
PRINTED IN THE UNITED STATES OF AMERICA

10 9 8 7 6 5 4 3 2 1

Contents

Foreword

In addition to writing the foreword for this edition of my father's *Tales of Lonely Trails*, I also had the rather considerable task of attempting to locate the old photographs or providing adequate substitutes for those already in the book. Although I was not able to find many of the old prints or negatives, I believe this new selection may be, in many ways, an improvement over the first volume and equal to the quality of those in my own book about my father, *Zane Grey: A Photographic Odyssey* (Taylor Publishing Company).

This collection of photographs also includes one of great historical significance. Originally misplaced in the old volume, but now restored to its proper position this is the close-up of Zane Grey and Nasja Begay, the Piute Indian who led the first white men (the 1909 Cummings/Wetherill expedition) to the Rainbow Bridge and then took my father and John Wetherill there in 1913. I came across this photograph somewhat by accident. In reading an account of the first visit to Rainbow Bridge in *National Parks Magazine,* I saw a photo cut of Nasja Begay's head; the caption read "courtesy of the National Archives." Not long after, I was looking through *Tales of Lonely Trails* and lo and behold, there was the same full picture. Under it, the caption read, "Which is the Piute?"

I suppose that this was probably the error of the layout editor, who had mistaken Begay for the Navajo guide, "Navvy," who was with my dad in 1907 on the first Buffalo Jones expedition into the Grand Canyon to rope wild mountain lions for sale to zoos. (Incidentally, Navvy's picture is reproduced for the first time in this volume.)

Perhaps another reason for the error is that in Zane Grey's story of his first trip to Nonnezoshe, which is the first story in this book, he called the Indian "Nas ta Bega." Later, in his novel, *The Rainbow Trail*, a sequel to *Riders of the Purple Sage*, Nas ta Bega becomes a Navajo chief and leads the major characters over the same trail that Dad and his party toiled across for so many hours to reach the bridge.

As is probably well known by now, Zane Grey had a penchant for renaming places and people when the original name was not to his liking. For example, the correct spelling of the Indian word for Rainbow Bridge is Nonnezochei, which he simplified to Nonnezoshe, by which it is known in most of the travel guides today. Similarly, the stretch of smooth granite mountains the party traversed to reach the bridge, mountains named the Slick Rocks by frontiersmen, were renamed by Zane Grey as the Glass Mountains. Later on, Arizona's Mogollon Rim became the Tonto Rim.

The historic importance of the photograph is enhanced because it is the only close-up of Nasja

Begay ever taken. He perished during the terrible
influenza epidemic of 1917–1918 that took the lives
of more than three thousand Indians on the Navajo
Reservation. However, his place in history is not
only assured by this photograph but also by the
plaque affixed to a stone near the south side of the
bridge, telling of his part in leading the explorers
there.

Otherwise, *Tales of Lonely Trails* is as it was
originally published, commencing with ZG's enthralling tale of his first visit to Nonnezoshe, and, in
Volume 2, ending with his description of the savage
wonders of Death Valley. Except for the books, *The
Last of the Plainsmen*, his story of Buffalo Jones,
and *Roping Lions in the Grand Canyon,* a portion of
which is contained here, this is the only non-fiction
book of Zane Grey's Western travels. It tells much
of the hardship, the toil, as well as the excitement
and thrill of hunting bear, deer, and wild turkey
throughout the then-primitive Western country, so
much of which he included in many of his novels. It
also tells a great deal about the frontiersmen who
were his guides and companions and prototypes for
many of the fascinating characters in his books.

I'm sure this book will be a valuable addition to
our understanding of how this magnificent country
came to inspire Zane Grey, as it has a host of others
both before and after him.

LOREN GREY
Woodland Hills, California

CHAPTER ONE

Nonnezoshe

John Wetherill, one of the famous Wetherill brothers and trader at Kayenta, Arizona, is the man who discovered Nonnezoshe, which is probably the most beautiful and wonderful natural phenomenon in the world. Wetherill owes the credit to his wife, who, through her influence with the Indians finally after years succeeded in getting the secret of the great bridge.

After three trips to Marsh Pass and Kayenta with my old guide, Al Doyle of Flagstaff, I finally succeeded in getting Wetherill to take me in to Nonnezoshe. This was in the spring of 1913 and my party was the second one, not scientific, to make the trip. Later this same year Wetherill took in the Roosevelt party and after that the Kolb brothers. It is a safe thing to say that this trip is one of the most beautiful in the West. It is a hard one and not for everybody. There is no guide except Wetherill, who knows how to get there. And after Doyle and I came out we admitted that we would not care to try to return over our back trail. We doubted if we could find the way.

This is the only place I have ever visited which I am not sure I could find again alone.

My trip to Nonnezoshe gave me the opportunity to see also Monument Valley, and the mysterious and labyrinthine Canyon Segi with its great prehistoric cliff-dwellings.

The desert beyond Kayenta spread out impressively, bare red flats and plains of sage leading to the rugged vividly-colored and wind-sculptored sandstone heights typical of the Painted Desert of Arizona. Laguna Creek, at that season, became flooded after every thunderstorm; and it was a treacherous red-mired quicksand where I convinced myself we would have stuck forever had it not been for Wetherill's Navajos.

We rode all day, for the most part closed in by ridges and bluffs, so that no extended view was possible. It was hot, too, and the sand blew and the dust rose. Travel in northern Arizona is never easy, and this grew harder and steeper. There was one long slope of heavy sand that I made sure would prove too much for Wetherill's pack mules. But they surmounted it apparently less breathless than I was. Toward sunset a storm gathered ahead of us to the north with a promise of cooling and sultry air.

At length we turned into a long canyon with straight rugged red walls, and a sandy floor with quite a perceptible ascent. It appeared endless. Far ahead I could see the black storm-clouds; and by and bye began to hear the rumble of thunder. Darkness had overtaken us by the time we had reached the head of this canyon; and my first sight of Monument Valley came with a dazzling flash of lightning. It revealed a vast valley, a strange world of colossal shafts and buttes of rock, magnificently sculptored, standing isolated and aloof, dark, weird, lonely. When the sheet lightning flared across the sky showing the monuments silhouetted black against that strange horizon the effect was marvelously beautiful. I watched until the storm died away.

Dawn, with the desert sunrise, changed Monument Valley, bereft it of its night gloom and weird shadow, and showed it in another aspect of beauty. It was hard for me to realize that those monuments were not the works of man. The great valley must once have been a plateau of red rock from which the softer strata had eroded, leaving the gentle league-long slopes marked here and there by upstanding pillars and columns of singular shape and beauty. I rode down the sweet-scented sageslopes under the shadow of the lofty Mittens, and around and across the valley, and back again to the height of land. And when I had completed the ride a story had woven itself into my mind; and the spot where I stood was to be the place where Lin Slone taught Lucy Bostil to ride the great stallion Wildfire.

Two days' ride took us across country to the Segi. With this wonderful canyon I was familiar, that is, as familiar as several visits could make a man with such a bewildering place. In fact I had named it Deception Pass. The Segi had innumerable branches, all more or less the same size, and sometimes it was difficult to tell the main canyon from one of its tributaries. The walls were rugged and crumbling, of a red or yellow hue, upward of a thousand feet in height, and indented by spruce-sided notches.

There were a number of ruined cliff-dwellings, the most accessible of which was Keet Seel. I could imagine no more picturesque spot. A huge wind-worn cavern with a vast slanted stained wall held upon a projecting ledge or shelf the long line of cliff-dwellings. These silent little stone houses with their vacant black eye-like windows had strange power to make me ponder, and then dream.

Next day, upon resuming our journey, it pleased me to try to find the trail to Betatakin, the most noted, and surely the most wonderful and beautiful ruin in all the West. In many places there was no trail at all, and I encountered difficulties, but in the end without much loss of time I entered the narrow rugged entrance of the canyon I had named Surprise Valley. Sight of the great dark cave thrilled me as I thought it might have thrilled Bess and Venters, who had lived for me their imagined lives of loneliness here in this wild spot. With the sight of those lofty walls and the scent of the dry sweet sage there rushed over me a strange feeling that "Riders of the Purple Sage" was true. My dream people of romance had really lived there once upon a time. I climbed high upon the huge stones, and along the smooth red walls where Fay Larkin once had glided with swift sure steps, and I entered the musty cliff-dwellings, and called out to hear the weird and sonorous echoes, and I wandered through the thickets and upon the grassy spruce-shaded benches, never for a moment free of the story I had conceived there. Something of awe and sadness abided with me. I could not enter into the merry pranks and investigations of my party. Surprise Valley seemed a part of my past, my dreams, my very self. I left it, haunted by its loneliness and silence and beauty, by the story it had given me.

That night we camped at Bubbling Spring, which once had been a geyser of considerable power. Wetherill told a story of an old Navajo who had lived there. For a long time, according to the Indian tale, the old chief resided there without complaining of this geyser that was wont to inundate his fields. But one season the unreliable waterspout made great and persistent endeavor to drown him and his people and horses. Whereupon the old Navajo took his gun and shot repeatedly at the geyser, and thundered aloud his anger to the Great Spirit. The geyser ebbed away, and from that day never burst forth again.

Somewhere under the great bulge of Navajo Mountain I calculated that we were coming to the edge of the plateau. The white bobbing pack-horses disappeared and then our extra mustangs. It is no unusual thing for a man to use three mounts on this trip. Then two of our Indians disappeared. But Wetherill waited for us and so did Nas ta Bega, the Piute who first took Wetherill down into Nonnezoshe Boco. As I came up I thought we had indeed reached the end of the world.

"It's down in there," said Wetherill, with a laugh.

Nas ta Bega made a slow sweeping gesture. There is always something so significant and impressive about an Indian when he points anywhere. It is as if he says, "There, way beyond, over the ranges, is a place I know, and it is far." The fact was that I looked at the Piute's dark, inscrutable face before I looked out into the void.

My gaze then seemed impelled and held by things afar, a vast yellow and purple corrugated world of distance, apparently now on a level with my eyes. I was drawn by the beauty and grandeur of that scene;

and then I was transfixed, almost by fear, by the realization that I dared to venture down into this wild and upflung fastness. I kept looking afar, sweeping the three-quarter circle of horizon till my judgment of distance was confounded and my sense of proportion dwarfed one moment and magnified the next.

Wetherill was pointing and explaining, but I had not grasped all he said.

"You can see two hundred miles into Utah," he went on. "That bright rough surface, like a washboard, is wind-worn rock. Those little lines of cleavage are canyons. There are a thousand canyons down there, and only a few have we been in. That long purple ragged line is the Grand Canyon of the Colorado. And there, that blue fork in the red, that's where the San Juan comes in. And there's Escalante Canyon."

I had to adopt the Indian's method of studying unlimited spaces in the desert—to look with slow contracted eyes from near to far.

The pack-train and the drivers had begun to zigzag down a long slope, bare of rock, with scant strips of green, and here and there a cedar. Half a mile down, the slope merged in what seemed a green level. But I knew it was not level. This level was a rolling plain, growing darker green, with lines of ravines and thin, undefined spaces that might be mirage. Miles and miles it swept and rolled and heaved, to lose its waves in apparent darker level. Round red rocks stood isolated. They resembled huge grazing cattle. But as I gazed these rocks were strangely magnified. They grew and grew into mounds, castles, domes, crags, great red wind-carved buttes. One by one they drew my gaze to the wall of upflung rock. I seemed to see a thousand domes of a thousand shapes and colors, and among them a thousand blue clefts, each of which was a canyon.

Beyond this wide area of curved lines rose another wall, dwarfing the lower; dark red, horizon-long, magnificent in frowning boldness, and because of its limitless deceiving surfaces incomprehensible to the gaze of man. Away to the eastward began a winding ragged blue line, looping back upon itself, and then winding away again, growing wider and bluer. This line was San Juan Canyon. I followed that blue line all its length, a hundred miles, down toward the west where it joined a dark purple shadowy cleft. And this was the Grand Canyon of the Colorado. My eye swept along with that winding mark, farther and farther to the west, until the cleft, growing larger and closer, revealed itself as a wild and winding canyon. Still farther westward it split a vast plateau of red peaks and yellow mesas. Here the canyon was full of purple smoke. It turned, it closed, it gaped, it lost itself and showed again in that chaos of a million cliffs. And then it faded, a mere purple line, into deceiving distance.

I imagined there was no scene in all the world to equal this. The tranquillity of lesser spaces was here not manifest. This happened to be a place where so much of the desert could be seen and the effect was stupendous. Sound, movement, life seemed to have no fitness here. Ruin was there and desolation and decay. The meaning of the ages was flung at me. A man became nothing. But when I gazed across that sublime and majestic wilderness, in which the Grand Canyon was only a dim line, I strangely lost my terror and something came to me across the shining spaces.

Then Nas ta Bega and Wetherill began the descent of the slope, and the rest of us followed. No sign of a trail showed where the base of the slope rolled out to meet the green plain. There was a level bench a mile wide, then a ravine, and then an ascent, and after that, rounded ridge and ravine, one after the other, like huge swells of a monstrous sea. Indian paint brush vied in its scarlet hue with the deep magenta of cactus. There was no sage. Soap weed and meager grass and a bunch of cactus here and there lent the green to that barren, and it was green only at a distance.

Nas ta Bega kept on at a steady gait. The sun climbed. The wind rose and whipped dust from under the mustangs. There is seldom much talk on a ride of this nature. It is hard work and everybody for himself. Besides, it is enough just to see; and that country is conducive to silence. I looked back often, and the farther out on the plain we rode the higher loomed the plateau we had descended; and as I faced ahead again, the lower sank the red-domed and castled horizon to the fore.

It was a wild place we were approaching. I saw piñon patches under the circled walls. I ceased to feel the dry wind in my face. We were already in the lee of a wall. I saw the rock squirrels scampering to their holes. Then the Indians disappeared between two rounded corners of cliff.

I rode round the corner into a widening space thick with cedars. It ended in a bare slope of smooth rock. Here we dismounted to begin the ascent. It was smooth and hard, though not slippery. There was not a crack. I did not see a broken piece of stone. Nas ta Bega and Wetherill climbed straight up for a while and then wound round a swell, to turn this way and that, always going up. I began to see similar mounds of rock all around me, of every shape that could be called a curve. There were yellow domes far above and small red domes far below. Ridges ran from one hill of rock to another. There were no abrupt breaks, but holes and pits and caves were everywhere, and occasionally deep down, an amphitheater green with cedar and piñon. We found no vestige of trail on those bare slopes.

Our guides led to the top of the wall, only to disclose to us another wall beyond, with a ridged, bare, and scalloped depression between. Here footing began to be precarious for both man and beast. Our mustangs were not shod and it was wonderful to see their slow, short, careful steps. They knew a great deal better than we what the danger was. It has been such experiences as this that have made me see in horses something besides beasts of burden. In the ascent of the second slope it was necessary to zigzag up, slowly and carefully, taking advantage of every bulge and depression.

Then before us twisted and dropped and curved the most dangerous slopes I had ever seen. We had reached the height of the divide and many of the drops on this side were perpendicular and too steep for us to see the bottom.

At one bad place Wetherill and Nas ta Bega, with Joe Lee, a Mormon cowboy with us, were helping one of the pack-horses named Chub. On the steepest part of this slope Chub fell and began to slide. His momentum jerked the rope from the hands of Wetherill and the Indian. But Joe Lee held on. Joe was a giant and being a Mormon he could not let go of anything he had. He began to slide with the horse, holding back with all his might.

It seemed that both man and beast must slide down to where the slope ended in a yawning precipice. Chub was snorting or screaming in terror. Our mustangs were frightened and rearing. It was not a place to have trouble with horses.

I had a moment of horrified fascination, in which Chub turned clear over. Then he slid into a little depression that, with Joe's hold on the lasso, momentarily checked his descent. Quick as thought Joe ran sidewise and down to the bulge of rock, and yelled for help. I got to him a little ahead of Wetherill and Nas ta Bega; and together we pulled Chub up out of danger. At first we thought he had been choked to death. But he came to, and got up, a bloody, skinned horse, but alive and safe. I have never seen a more magnificent effort than Joe Lee's. Those fellows are built that way. Wetherill has lost horses on those treacherous slopes, and that risk is the only thing about the trip which is not splendid.

We got over that bad place without further incident, and presently came to a long swell of naked stone that led down to a narrow green split. This one had straight walls and wound away out of sight. It was the head of a canyon.

"Nonnezoshe Boco," said the Indian.

This then was the Canyon of the Rainbow Bridge. When we got down into it we were a happy crowd. The mode of travel here was a selection of the best levels, the best places to cross the brook, the best places to climb, and it was a process of continual repetition. Thre was no trail ahead of us, but we certainly left one behind. And as Wetherill picked out the course and the mustangs followed him I had all freedom to see and feel the beauty, color, wildness and changing character of Nonnezoshe Boco.

My experiences in the desert did not count much in the trip down this strange, beautiful lost canyon. All canyons are not alike. This one did not widen, though the walls grew higher. They began to lean and bulge, and the narrow strip of sky above resembled a flowing blue river. Huge caverns had been hollowed out by water or wind. And when the brook ran close under one of these overhanging places the running water made a singular indescribable sound. A crack from a hoof on a stone rang like a hollow bell and echoed from wall to wall. And the croak of a frog—the only living creature I noted in the canyon—was a weird and melancholy thing.

"We're sure gettin' deep down," said Joe Lee.

"How do you know?" I asked.

"Here are the pink and yellow sego lilies. Only the white ones are found above."

I dismounted to gather some of these lilies. They were larger than the white ones of higher altitudes, of a most exquisite beauty and fragility, and of such rare pink and yellow hues as I had never seen.

"They bloom only where it's always summer," explained Joe.

That expressed their nature. They were the orchids of the summer canyons. They stood up everywhere star-like out of the green. It was impossible to prevent the mustangs treading them under foot. And as the canyon deepened, and many little springs added their tiny volume to the brook, every grassy bench was dotted with lilies, like a green sky star-spangled. And this increasing luxuriance manifested itself in the banks of purple moss and clumps of lavender daisies and great mounds of yellow violets. The brook was lined by blossoming buck-brush; the rocky corners showed the crimson and magenta of cactus; and there were ledges of green with shining moss that sparkled with little white flowers. The hum of bees filled the fragrant, dreamy air.

But by and bye, this green and colorful and verdant beauty, the almost level floor of the canyon, the banks of soft earth, the thickets and clumps of cottonwood, the shelving caverns and bulging walls—these features were gradually lost, and Nonnezoshe began to deepen in bare red and white stone steps. The walls sheered away from one another, breaking into sections and ledges, and rising higher and higher, and there began to be manifested a dark and solemn concordance with the nature that had created this old rent in the earth.

There was a stretch of miles where steep steps in hard red rock alternated with long levels of round boulders. Here, one by one, the mustangs went lame and we had to walk. And we slipped and stumbled along over these loose, treacherous stones. The hours passed; the toil increased; the progress diminished; one of the mustangs failed and was left. And all the while the dimensions of Nonnezoshe Boco magnified and its character changed. It became a thousand-foot walled canyon, leaning, broken, threatening, with great yellow slides blocking passage, with huge sections split off from the main wall, with immense dark and gloomy caverns. Strangely it had no intersecting canyons. It jealously guarded its secret. Its unusual formations of cavern and pillar and half-arch led me to expect any monstrous stone-shape left by avalanche or cataclysm.

Down and down we toiled. And now the stream-bed was bare of boulders and the banks of earth. The floods that had rolled down that canyon had here borne away every loose thing. All the floor, in places, was bare red and white stone, polished, glistening, slippery, affording treacherous foothold. And the time came when Wetherill abandoned the stream-bed to take to the rock-strewn and cactus-covered ledges above.

The canyon widened ahead into a great ragged iron-lined amphitheater, and then apparently turned abruptly at right angles. Sunset rimmed the walls.

I had been tired for a long time and now I began to limp and lag. I wondered what on earth would make Wetherill and the Indians tired. It was with great pleasure that I observed the giant Joe Lee plodding slowly along. And when I glanced behind at my straggling party it was with both admiration for their gameness and glee for their disheveled and weary appearance. Finally I got so that all I could do was to drag myself onward with eyes down on the rough ground. In this way I kept on until I heard Wetherill call me. He had stopped—was waiting for me. The dark and silent Indian stood beside him, looking down the canyon.

I saw past the vast jutting wall that had obstructed my view. A mile beyond, all was bright with the colors of sunset, and spanning the canyon in the graceful shape and beautiful hues of the rainbow was a magnificent natural bridge.

"Nonnezoshe," said Wetherill, simply.

This rainbow bridge was the one great natural phenomenon, the one grand spectacle which I had ever seen that did not at first give vague disappointment, a confounding of reality, a disenchantment of contrast with what the mind had conceived.

But this thing was glorious. It absolutely silenced me. My body and brain, weary and dull from the toil of travel, received a singular and revivifying freshness. I had a strange, mystic perception that this rosy-hued, tremendous arch of stone was a goal I had failed to reach in some former life, but had now found. Here was a rainbow magnified even beyond dreams, a thing not transparent and ethereal, but solidified, a work of ages, sweeping up majestically from the red walls, its iris-hued arch against the blue sky.

Then we plodded on again. Wetherill worked around to circle the huge amphitheater. The way was a steep slant, rough and loose and dragging. The rocks were as hard and jagged as lava, and cactus hindered progress. Soon the rosy and golden lights had faded. All the walls turned pale and steely and the bridge loomed dark.

We were to camp all night under the bridge. Just before we reached it Nas ta Bega halted with one of his singular motions. He was saying his prayer to this great stone god. Then he began to climb straight up the steep slope. Wetherill told me the Indian would not pass under the arch.

When we got to the bridge and unsaddled and unpacked the lame mustangs twilight had fallen. The horses were turned loose to fare for what scant grass grew on bench and slope. Firewood was even harder to find than grass. When our simple meal had been eaten there was gloom gathering in the canyon and stars had begun to blink in the pale strip of blue above the lofty walls. The place was oppressive and we were mostly silent.

Presently I moved away into the strange dark shadow cast by the bridge. It was a weird black belt, where I imagined I was invisible, but out of which I could see. There was a slab of rock upon which I composed myself, to watch, to feel.

A stiffening of my neck made me aware that I had been continually looking up at the looming arch. I found that it never seemed the same any two moments. Near at hand it was too vast a thing for immediate comprehension. I wanted to ponder on what had formed it—to reflect upon its meaning as to age and force of nature. Yet it seemed that all I could do was to see. White stars hung along the dark curved line. The rim of the arch appeared to shine. The moon was up there somewhere. The far side of the canyon was now a blank black wall. Over its towering rim showed a pale glow. It brightened. The shades in the canyon lightened, then a white disk of moon peeped over the dark line. The bridge turned to silver.

It was then that I became aware of the presence of Nas ta Bega. Dark, silent, statuesque, with inscrutable face uplifted, with all that was spiritual of the Indian suggested by a somber and tranquil knowledge of his place there, he represented to me that which a solitary figure of human life represents in a great painting. Nonnezoshe needed life, wild life, life of its millions of years—and here stood the dark and silent Indian.

Long afterward I walked there alone, to and fro,

under the bridge. The moon had long since crossed the streak of star-fired blue above, and the canyon was black in shadow. At times a current of wind, with all the strangeness of that strange country in its moan, rushed through the great stone arch. At other times there was silence such as I imagined might have dwelt deep in the center of the earth. And again an owl hooted, and the sound was nameless. It had a mocking echo. An echo of night, silence, gloom, melancholy, death, age, eternity!

The Indian lay asleep with his dark face upturned, and the other sleepers lay calm and white in the starlight. I seemed to see in them the meaning of life and the past—the illimitable train of faces that had shone under the stars. There was something nameless in that canyon, and whether or not it was what the Indian embodied in the great Nonnezoshe, or the life of the present, or the death of the ages, or the nature so magnificently manifested in those silent, dreaming, waiting walls—the truth was that there was a spirit.

I did sleep a few hours under Nonnezoshe, and when I awoke the tip of the arch was losing its cold darkness and beginning to shine. The sun had just risen high enough over some low break in the wall to reach the bridge. I watched. Slowly, in wondrous transformation, the gold and blue and rose and pink and purple blended their hues, softly, mistily, cloud-ily, until once more the arch was a rainbow.

I realized that long before life had evolved upon the earth this bridge had spread its grand arch from wall to wall, black and mystic at night, transparent and rosy in the sunrise, at sunset a flaming curve limned against the heavens. When the race of man had passed it would, perhaps, stand there still. It was not for many eyes to see. The tourist, the leisurely traveler, the comfort-loving motorist would never behold it. Only by toil, sweat, endurance and pain could any man ever look at Nonnezoshe. It seemed well to realize that the great things of life had to be earned. Nonnezoshe would always be alone, grand, silent, beautiful, unintelligible; and as such I bade it a mute, reverent farewell.

CHAPTER TWO

Colorado Trails

Riding and tramping trails would lose half their charm if the motive were only to hunt and to fish. It seems fair to warn the reader who longs to embark upon a bloody game hunt or a chronicle of fishing records that this is not that kind of story. But it will be one for those who love horses and dogs, the long winding dim trails, the wild flowers and the dark still woods, the fragrance of spruce and the smell of camp-fire smoke. And as well for those who love to angle in brown lakes or rushing brooks or chase after the baying hounds or stalk the stag on his lonely heights.

We left Denver on August twenty-second over the Moffet road and had a long wonderful ride through the mountains. The Rockies have a sweep, a limitless sweep, majestic and grand. For many miles we crossed no streams, and climbed and wound up barren slopes. Once across the divide, however, we descended into a country of black forests and green valleys. Yampa, a little hamlet with a past prosperity, lay in the wide valley of the Bear River. It was picturesque but idle, and a better name for it would have been Sleepy Hollow. The main and only street was very wide and dusty, bordered by old board walks and vacant stores. It seemed a deserted street of a deserted village. Teague, the guide, lived there. He assured me it was not quite as lively a place as in the early days when it was a stage center for an old and rich mining section. We stayed there at the one hotel for a whole day, most of which I spent sitting on the board walk. Whenever I chanced to look down the wide street it seemed always the same— deserted. But Yampa had the charm of being old and forgotten, and for that reason I would like to live there a while.

On August twenty-third we started in two buck-boards for the foothills, some fifteen miles west-ward, where Teague's men were to meet us with saddle and pack horses. The ride was not interesting until the Flattop Mountains began to loom, and we saw the dark green slopes of spruce, rising to bare gray cliffs and domes, spotted with white banks of snow. I felt the first cool breath of mountain air, exhilarating and sweet. From that moment I began to live.

We had left at six-thirty. Teague, my guide, had been so rushed with his manifold tasks that I had scarcely seen him, let alone gotten acquainted with him. And on this ride he was far behind with our load of baggage. We arrived at the edge of the foothills about noon. It appeared to be the gateway of a valley, with aspen groves and ragged jack-pines on the slopes, and a stream running down. Our driver called it the Stillwater. That struck me as strange, for the stream was in a great hurry. R. C. spied trout in it, and schools of darkish, mullet-like

fish which we were informed were grayling. We
wished for our tackle then and for time to fish.

Teague's man, a young fellow called Virgil, met
us here. He did not resemble the ancient Virgil in the
least, but he did look as if he had walked right out of
one of my romances of wild riders. So I took a liking
to him at once.

But the bunch of horses he had corralled there did
not excite any delight in me. Horses, of course, were
the most important part of our outfit. And that moment of first seeing the horses that were to carry us
on such long rides was an anxious and thrilling one.
I have felt it many times, and it never grows any
weaker from experience. Many a scrubby lot of
horses had turned out well upon acquaintance, and
some I had found hard to part with at the end of
trips. Up to that time, however, I had not seen a bear
hunter's horses; and I was much concerned by the
fact that these were a sorry looking outfit, dusty,
ragged, maneless, cut and bruised and crippled. Still,
I reflected, they were bunched up so closely that I
could not tell much about them, and I decided to
wait for Teague before I chose a horse for any one.

In an hour Teague trotted up to our resting place.
Beside his own mount he had two white saddle
horses, and nine pack-animals, heavily laden. Teague
was a sturdy rugged man with bronzed face and keen
gray-blue eyes, very genial and humorous. Straightway I got the impression that he liked work.

"Let's organize," he said, briskly. "Have you
picked the horses you're goin' to ride?"

Teague led from the midst of that dusty kicking
bunch a rangy powerful horse, with four white feet,

a white face and a noble head. He had escaped my eye. I felt thrillingly that here at least was one horse.

The rest of the horses were permanently crippled or temporarily lame, and I had no choice, except to take the one it would be kindest to ride.

"He ain't much like your Silvermane or Black Star," said Teague, laughing.

"What do you know about them?" I asked, very much pleased at this from him.

"Well, I know all about them," he replied. "I'll have you the best horse in this country in a few days. Fact is I've bought him, an' he'll come with my cowboy, Vern. . . . Now, we're organized. Let's move."

We rode through a meadow along a spruce slope above which towered the great mountain. It was a zigzag trail, rough, boggy, and steep in places. The Stillwater meandered here, and little breaks on the water gave evidence of feeding trout. We had several miles of meadow, and then sheered off to the left up into the timber. It was a spruce forest, very still and fragrant. We climbed out up on a bench, and across a flat, up another bench, out of the timber into the patches of snow. Here snow could be felt in the air. Water was everywhere. I saw a fox, a badger, and another furry creature, too illusive to name. One more climb brought us to the top of the Flattop Pass, about eleven thousand feet. The view in the direction from which we had come was splendid, and led the eye to the distant sweeping ranges, dark and dim along the horizon. The Flattops were flat enough, but not very wide at this pass, and we were soon going down again into a green gulf of spruce, with ragged peaks lifting beyond. Here again I got

the suggestion of limitless space. It took us an hour
to ride down to Little Trappers Lake, a small clear
green sheet of water. The larger lake was farther
down. It was big, irregular, and bordered by spruce
forests, and shadowed by the lofty gray peaks.

The Camp was on the far side. The air appeared
rather warm, and mosquitoes bothered us. However,
they did not stay long. It was after sunset and I was
too tired to have many impressions.

Our cook appeared to be a melancholy man. He
had a deep quavering voice, a long drooping mus-
tache and sad eyes. He was silent most of the time.
The men called him Bill, and yelled when they
spoke, for he was somewhat deaf. It did not take me
long to discover that he was a good cook.

Our tent was pitched down the slope from the
cook tent. We were too tired to sit round a camp-fire
and talk. The stars were white and splendid, and
they hung over the flat ridges like great beacon
lights. The lake appeared to be inclosed on three
sides by amphitheatric mountains, black with spruce
up to the gray walls of rock. The night grew cold
and very still. The bells on the horses tinkled dis-
tantly. There was a soft murmur of falling water. A
lonesome coyote barked, and that thrilled me. Teague's
dogs answered this prowler, and some of them had
voices to make a hunter thrill. One, the bloodhound
Cain, had a roar like a lion's. I had not gotten
acquainted with the hounds, and I was thinking about
them when I fell asleep.

Next morning I was up at five-thirty. The air was
cold and nipping and frost shone on grass and sage.
A red glow of sunrise gleamed on the tip of the
mountain and slowly grew downward.

The cool handle of an axe felt good. I soon found, however, that I could not wield it long for lack of breath. The elevation was close to ten thousand feet and the air at that height was thin and rare. After each series of lusty strokes I had to rest. R. C., who could handle an axe as he used to swing a baseball bat, made fun of my efforts. Whereupon I relinquished the tool to him, and chuckled at his discomfiture.

After breakfast R. C. and I got out our tackles and rigged up fly rods, and sallied forth to the lake with the same eagerness we had felt when we were boys going after chubs and sunfish. The lake glistened green in the sunlight and it lay like a gem at the foot of the magnificent black slopes.

The water was full of little floating particles that Teague called wild rice. I thought the lake had begun to work, like eastern lakes during dog days. It did not look propitious for fishing, but Teague reassured us. The outlet of this lake was the head of White River. We tried the outlet first, but trout were not rising there. Then we began wading and casting along a shallow bar of the lake. Teague had instructed us to cast, then drag the flies slowly across the surface of the water, in imitation of a swimming fly or bug. I tried this, and several times, when the leader was close to me and my rod far back, I had strikes. With my rod in that position I could not hook the trout. Then I cast my own way, letting the flies sink a little. To my surprise and dismay I had only a few strikes and could not hook the fish.

R. C., however, had better luck, and that too in wading right over the ground I had covered. To beat me at anything always gave him the most unaccountable fiendish pleasure.

"These are educated trout," he said. "It takes a skillful fisherman to make them rise. Now anybody can catch the big game of the sea, which is your forte. But here you are N. G. . . . Watch me cast!"

I watched him make a most atrocious cast. But the water boiled, and he hooked two good-sized trout at once. Quite speechless with envy and admiration I watched him play them and eventually beach them. They were cutthroat trout, silvery-sided and marked with the red slash along their gills that gave them their name. I did not catch any while wading, but from the bank I spied one, and dropping a fly in front of his nose, I got him. R. C. caught four more, all about a pound in weight, and then he had a strike that broke his leader. He did not have another leader, so we walked back to camp.

Wild flowers colored the open slopes leading down out of the forest. Golden rod, golden daisies, and bluebells were plentiful and very pretty. Here I found my first columbine, the beautiful flower that is the emblem of Colorado. In vivid contrast to its blue, Indian paint brush thinly dotted the slopes and varied in color from red to pink and from white to yellow.

My favorite of all wild flowers—the purple asters—were there too, on tall nodding stems, with pale faces held up to the light. The reflection of mountain and forest in Trappers Lake was clear and beautiful.

The hounds bayed our approach to camp. We both made a great show about beginning our little camp tasks, but we did not last very long. The sun felt so good and it was so pleasant to lounge under a pine. One of the blessings of outdoor life was that a man

could be like an Indian and do nothing. So from rest
I passed to dreams and from dreams to sleep.

In the afternoon R. C. and I went out again to try
for trout. The lake appeared to be getting thicker
with that floating muck and we could not raise a
fish. Then we tried the outlet again. Here the current
was swift. I found a place between two willow banks
where trout were breaking on the surface. It took a
long cast for me, but about every tenth attempt I
would get a fly over the right place and raise a fish.
They were small, but that did not detract from my
gratification. The light on the water was just right
for me to see the trout rise, and that was a beautiful
sight as well as a distinct advantage. I had caught
four when a shout from R. C. called me quickly
down stream. I found him standing in the middle of
a swift chute with his rod bent double and a long line
out.

"Got a whale!" he yelled. "See him—down
there—in that white water. See him flash red! . . .
Go down there and land him for me. Hurry! He's got
all the line!"

I ran below to an open place in the willows. Here
the stream was shallow and very swift. In the white
water I caught a flashing gleam of red. Then I saw
the shine of the leader. But I could not reach it
without wading in. When I did this the trout lunged
out. He looked crimson and silver. I could have put
my fist in his mouth.

"Grab the leader! Yank him out!" yelled R. C. in
desperation. "There! He's got all the line."

"But it'd be better to wade down," I yelled back.

He shouted that the water was too deep and for me
to save his fish. This was an awful predicament for

me. I knew the instant I grasped the leader that the
big trout would break it or pull free. The same
situation, with different kinds of fish, had presented
itself many times on my numberless fishing jaunts
with R. C. and they all crowded to my mind. Nevertheless I had no choice. Plunging in to my knees I
frantically reached for the leader. The red trout made
a surge. I missed him. R. C. yelled that something
would break. That was no news to me. Another
plunge brought me in touch with the leader. Then I
essayed to lead the huge cutthroat ashore. He was
heavy. But he was tired and that gave birth to hopes.
Near the shore as I was about to lift him he woke up,
swam round me twice, then ran between my legs.

When, a little later, R. C. came panting down
stream I was sitting on the bank, all wet, with one
knee skinned and I was holding his broken leader in
my hands. Strange to say, he went into a rage!
Blamed me for the loss of that big trout! Under such
circumstances it was always best to maintain silence
and I did so as long as I could. After his paroxysm
had spent itself and he had become somewhat near a
rational being once more he asked me:

"Was he big?"

"Oh—a whale of a trout!" I replied.

"Humph! Well, how big?"

Thereupon I enlarged upon the exceeding size and
beauty of that trout. I made him out very much
bigger than he actually looked to me and I minutely
described his beauty and wonderful gaping mouth.
R. C. groaned and that was my revenge.

We returned to camp early, and I took occasion to
scrape acquaintance with the dogs. It was a strangely
assorted pack—four Airedales, one bloodhound and

seven other hounds of mixed breeds. There were also three pup hounds, white and yellow, very pretty dogs, and like all pups, noisy and mischievous. They made friends easily. This applied also to one of the Airedales, a dog recently presented to Teague by some estimable old lady who had called him Kaiser and made a pet of him. As might have been expected of a dog, even an Airedale, with that name, he was no good. But he was very affectionate, and exceedingly funny. When he was approached he had a trick of standing up, holding up his forepaws in an appealing sort of way, with his head twisted in the most absurd manner. This was when he was chained—otherwise he would have been climbing up on any one who gave him the chance. He was the most jealous dog I ever saw. He could not be kept chained very long because he always freed himself. At meal time he would slip noiselessly behind some one and steal the first morsel he could snatch. Bill was always rapping Kaiser with pans or billets of firewood.

Next morning was clear and cold. We had breakfast, and then saddled up to ride to Big Fish Lake. For an hour we rode up and down ridges of heavy spruce, along a trail. We saw elk and deer sign. Elk tracks appeared almost as large as cow tracks. When we left the trail to climb into heavy timber we began to look for game. The forest was dark, green and brown, silent as a grave. No squirrels or birds or sign of life! We had a hard ride up and down steep slopes. A feature was the open swaths made by avalanches. The ice and snow had cut a path through the timber, and the young shoots of spruce were springing up. I imagined the roar made by that tremendous slide.

We found elk tracks everywhere and some fresh sign, where the grass had been turned recently, and also much old and fresh sign where the elk had skinned the saplings by rubbing their antlers to get rid of the velvet. Some of these rubs looked like blazes made by an axe. The Airedale Fox, a wonderful dog, routed out a she-coyote that evidently had a den somewhere, for she barked angrily at the dog and at us. Fox could not catch her. She led him round in a circle, and we could not see her in the thick brush. It was fine to hear the wild staccato note again.

We crossed many little parks, bright and green, blooming with wild asters and Indian paint brush and golden daisies. The patches of red and purple were exceedingly beautiful. Everywhere we rode we were knee deep in flowers. At length we came out of the heavy timber down upon Big Fish Lake. This lake was about half a mile across, deep blue-green in color, with rocky shores. Upon the opposite side were beaver mounds. We could see big trout swimming round, but they would not rise to a fly. R. C. went out in an old boat and paddled to the head of the lake and fished at the inlet. Here he caught a fine trout. I went around and up the little river that fed the lake. It curved swiftly through a meadow, and had deep, dark eddies under mossy, flowering banks. At other places the stream ran swiftly over clean gravel beds. It was musical and clear as crystal, and to the touch of hand, as cold as ice water. I waded in and began to cast. I saw several big trout, and at last coaxed one to take my fly. But I missed him. Then in a swift current a flash of red caught my eye and I saw a big trout lazily rise to my fly. Saw him take it!

And I hooked him. He was not active, but heavy and plunging, and he bored in and out, and made short runs. I had not seen such beautiful red colors in any fish. He made a fine fight, but at last I landed him on the grass, a cutthroat of about one and three-quarter pounds, deep red and silver and green, and spotted all over. That was the extent of my luck.

We went back to the point, and thought we would wait a little while to see if the trout would begin to rise. But they did not. A storm began to mutter and boom along the battlements. Great gray clouds obscured the peaks, and at length the rain came. It was cold and cutting. We sought the shelter of spruces for a while, and waited. After an hour it cleared somewhat, and R. C. caught a fine one-pound cutthroat, all green and silver, with only two slashes of red along under the gills. Then another storm threatened. Before we got ready to leave for camp the rain began again to fall, and we looked for a wetting. It was raining hard when we rode into the woods and very cold. The spruces were dripping. But we soon got warm from hard riding up steep slopes. After an hour the rain ceased, the sun came out, and from the open places high up we could see a great green void of spruce, and beyond, boundless black ranges, running off to dim horizon. We flushed a big blue grouse with a brood of little ones, and at length another big one.

In one of the open parks the Airedale Fox showed signs of scenting game. There was a patch of ground where the grass was pressed down. Teague whispered and pointed. I saw the gray rump of an elk protruding from behind some spruces. I beckoned for R. C. and we both dismounted. Just then the elk rose and stalked out. It was a magnificent bull with crowning lofty antlers. The shoulders and neck appeared black. He raised his head, and turning, trotted away with ease and grace for such a huge beast. That was a wild and beautiful sight I had not seen before. We were entranced, and when he disappeared, we burst out with exclamations.

We rode on toward camp, and out upon a bench that bordered the lofty red wall of rock. From there we went down into heavy forest again, dim and gray, with its dank, penetrating odor, and oppressive stillness. The forest primeval! When we rode out of that into open slopes the afternoon was far advanced, and long shadows lay across the distant ranges. When we reached camp, supper and a fire to warm cold wet feet were exceedingly welcome. I was tired.

Later, R. C. and I rode up a mile or so above camp, and hitched our horses near Teague's old corral. Our intention was to hunt up along the side of the slope. Teague came along presently. We waited, hoping the big black clouds would break. But they did not. They rolled down with gray, swirling edges, like smoke, and a storm enveloped us. We sought shelter in a thick spruce. It rained and hailed. By and bye the air grew bitterly cold, and Teague suggested we give up, and ride back. So we did. The mountains were dim and obscure through the gray gloom, and the black spear-tipped spruces looked ghostly against the background. The lightning was vivid, and the thunder rolled and crashed in magnificent bombardment across the heavens.

Next morning at six-thirty the sun was shining clear, and only a few clouds sailed in the blue. Wind was in the west and the weather promised fair. But

clouds began to creep up behind the mountains, first
hazy, then white, then dark. Nevertheless we decided to ride out, and cross the Flattop rim, and go
around what they call the Chinese Wall. It rained as
we climbed through the spruces above Little Trappers Lake. And as we got near the top it began to
hail. Again the air grew cold. Once out on top I
found a wide expanse, green and white, level in
places, but with huge upheavals of ridge. There were
flowers here at eleven thousand feet. The view to the
rear was impressive—a wide up-and-down plain studded with out-cropping of rocks, and patches of snow.
We were then on top of the Chinese Wall, and the
view to the west was grand. At the moment hail was
falling thick and white, and to stand above the streaked
curtain, as it fell into the abyss was a strange new
experience. Below, two thousand feet, lay the spruce
forest, and it sloped and dropped into the White
River Valley, which in turn rose, a long ragged
dark-green slope, up to a bare jagged peak. Beyond
this stretched range on range, dark under the lowering pall of clouds. On top we found fresh Rocky
Mountain sheep tracks. A little later, going into a
draw, we crossed a snow-bank, solid as ice. We
worked down into this draw into the timber. It hailed,
and rained some more, then cleared. The warm sun
felt good. Once down in the parks we began to ride
through a flower-garden. Every slope was beautiful
in gold, and red, and blue and white. These parks
were luxuriant with grass, and everywhere we found
elk beds, where the great stags had been lying, to
flee at our approach. But we did not see one. The
bigness of this slope impressed me. We rode miles
and miles, and every park was surrounded by heavy

timber. At length we got into a burned district where
the tall dead spruces stood sear and ghastly, and the
ground was so thickly strewn with fallen trees that
we had difficulty in threading a way through them.
Patches of aspen grew on the hillside, still fresh and
green despite this frosty morning. Here we found a
sego lily, one of the most beautiful of flowers. Here
also I saw pink Indian paint brush. At the foot of this
long burned slope we came to the White River trail,
and followed it up and around to camp.

Late in the evening, about sunset, I took my rifle
and slipped off into the woods back of camp. I
walked a short distance, then paused to listen to the
silence of the forest. There was not a sound. It was a
place of peace. By and bye I heard snapping of
twigs, and presently heard R. C. and Teague approaching me. We penetrated half a mile into the
spruce, pausing now and then to listen. At length
R. C. heard something. We stopped. After a little I
heard the ring of a horn on wood. It was thrilling.
Then came the crack of a hoof on stone, then the
clatter of a loosened rock. We crept on. But that elk
or deer evaded us. We hunted around till dark without farther sign of any game.

R. C. and Teague and I rode out at seven-thirty
and went down White River for three miles. In one
patch of bare ground we saw tracks of five deer
where they had come in for salt. Then we climbed
high up a burned ridge, winding through patches of
aspen. We climbed ridge after ridge, and at last got
out of the burned district into reaches of heavy spruce.
Coming to a park full of deer and elk tracks, we
dismounted and left our horses. I went to the left,
and into some beautiful woods, where I saw beds of

deer or elk, and many tracks. Returning to the horses, I led them into a larger park, and climbed high into the open and watched. There I saw some little squirrels about three inches long, and some gray birds, very tame. I waited a long time before there was any sign of R. C. or Teague, and then it was the dog I saw first. I whistled, and they climbed up to me. We mounted and rode on for an hour, then climbed through a magnificent forest of huge trees, windfalls, and a ferny, mossy, soft ground. At length we came out at the head of a steep, bare slope, running down to a verdant park crossed by stretches of timber. On the way back to camp we ran across many elk beds and deer trails, and for a while a small band of elk evidently trotted ahead of us, but out of sight.

Next day we started for a few days' trip to Big Fish Lake. R. C. and I went along up around the mountain. I found our old trail, and was at a loss only a few times. We saw fresh elk sign, but no live game at all.

In the afternoon we fished. I went up the river half a mile, while R. C. fished the lake. Neither of us had any luck. Later we caught four trout, one of which was fair sized.

Toward sunset the trout began to rise all over the lake, but we could not get them to take a fly.

The following day we went up to Twin Lakes and found them to be beautiful little green gems surrounded by spruce. I saw some big trout in the large lake, but they were wary. We tried every way to get a strike. No use! In the little lake matters were worse. It was full of trout up to two pounds. They would run at the fly, only to refuse it. Exasperating work! We gave up and returned to Big Fish. After supper we went out to try again. The lake was smooth and quiet. All at once, as if by concert, the trout began to rise everywhere. In a little bay we began to get strikes. I could see the fish rise to the fly. The small ones were too swift and the large ones too slow, it seemed. We caught one, and then had bad luck. We snarled our lines, drifted wrong, broke leaders, snapped off flies, hooked too quick and too slow, and did everything that was clumsy. I lost two big fish because they followed the fly as I drew it toward me across the water to imitate a swimming fly. Of course this made a large slack line which I could not get up. Finally I caught one big fish, and altogether we got seven. All in that little bay, where the water was shallow! In other places we could not catch a fish. I had one vicious strike. The fish appeared to be feeding on a tiny black gnat, which we could not imitate. This was the most trying experience of all. We ought to have caught a basketful.

The next day, September first, we rode down along the outlet of Big Fish to White River and down that for miles to fish for grayling. The stream was large and swift and cold. It appeared full of ice water and rocks, but no fish. We met fishermen, an automobile, and a camp outfit. That was enough for me. Where an automobile can run, I do not belong. The fishing was poor. But the beautiful open valley, flowered in gold and purple, was recompense for a good deal of bad luck.

A grayling, or what they called a grayling, was not as beautiful a fish as my fancy had pictured. He resembled a sucker or mullet, had a small mouth, dark color, and was rather a sluggish-looking fish.

We rode back through a thunderstorm, and our yellow slickers afforded much comfort.

Next morning was bright, clear, cold. I saw the moon go down over a mountain rim rose-flushed with the sunrise.

R. C. and I, with Teague, started for the top of the big mountain on the west. I had a new horse, a roan, and he looked a thoroughbred. He appeared tired. But I thought he would be great. We took a trail through the woods, dark green-gray, cool and verdant, odorous and still. We began to climb. Occasionally we crossed parks, and little streams. Up near the long, bare slope the spruce trees grew large and far apart. They were beautiful, gray as if bearded with moss. Beyond this we got into the rocks and climbing became arduous. Long zigzags up the slope brought us to the top of a notch, where at the right lay a patch of snow. The top of the mountain was comparatively flat, but it had timbered ridges and bare plains and little lakes, with dark domes, rising beyond. We rode around to the right, climbing out of the timber to where the dwarf spruces and brush had a hard struggle for life. The great gulf below us was immense, dark, and wild, studded with lakes and parks, and shadowed by moving clouds.

Sheep tracks, old and fresh, afforded us thrills.

Away on the western rim, where we could look down upon a long rugged iron-gray ridge of mountain, our guide using the glass, found two big stags. We all had our fill of looking. I could see them plainly with naked eyes.

We decided to go back to where we could climb down on that side, halter the horses, leave all extra accoutrements, and stalk those stags, and take a picture of them.

I led the way, and descended under the rim. It was up and down over rough shale, and up steps of broken rocks, and down little cliffs. We crossed the ridge twice, many times having to lend a hand to each other.

At length I reached a point where I could see the stags lying down. The place was an open spot on a rocky promontory with a fringe of low spruces. The stags were magnificent in size, with antlers in the velvet. One had twelve points. They were lying in the sun to harden their horns, according to our guide.

I slipped back to the others, and we all decided to have a look. So we climbed up. All of us saw the stags, twitching ears and tails.

Then we crept back, and once more I took the lead to crawl round under the ledge so we could come up about even with them. Here I found the hardest going yet. I came to a wind-worn crack in the thin ledge, and from this I could just see the tips of the antlers. I beckoned the others. Laboriously they climbed. R. C. went through first. I went over next, and then came Teague.

R. C. and I started to crawl down to a big rock that was our objective point. We went cautiously, with bated breath and pounding hearts. When we got there I peeped over to see the stags still lying down. But they had heads intent and wary. Still I did not think they had scented us. R. C. took a peep, and turning excitedly he whispered:

"See only one. And he's standing!"

And I answered: " Let's get down around to the

left where we can get a better chance." It was only a few feet down. We got there.

When he peeped over at this point he exclaimed: "They're gone!"

It was a keen disappointment. "They winded us," I decided.

We looked and looked. But we could not see to our left because of the bulge of rock. We climbed back. Then I saw one of the stags loping leisurely off to the left. Teague was calling. He said they had walked off the promontory, looking up, and stopping occasionally.

Then we realized we must climb back along that broken ridge and then up to the summit of the mountain. So we started.

That climb back was proof of the effect of excitement on judgment. We had not calculated at all on the distance or ruggedness, and we had a job before us. We got along well under the western wall, and fairly well straight across through the long slope of timber, where we saw sheep tracks, and expected any moment to sight an old ram. But we did not find one, and when we got out of the timber upon the bare sliding slope we had to halt a hundred times. We could zigzag only a few steps. The altitude was twelve thousand feet, and oxygen seemed scarce. I nearly dropped. All the climbing appeared to come hardest on the middle of my right foot, and it could scarcely have burned hotter if it had been in fire. Despite the strenuous toil there were not many moments that I was not aware of the vastness of the gulf below, or the peaceful lakes, brown as amber, or the golden parks. And nearer at hand I found magenta-colored Indian paint brush, very exquisite and rare.

Coming out on a ledge I spied a little, dark animal with a long tail. He was running along the opposite promontory about three hundred yards distant. When he stopped I took a shot at him and missed by apparently a scant half foot.

After catching our breath we climbed more and more, and still more, at last to drop on the rim, hot, wet and utterly spent.

The air was keen, cold, and invigorating. We were soon rested, and finding our horses we proceeded along the rim westward. Upon rounding an outcropping of rock we flushed a flock of ptarmigan— soft gray, rock-colored birds about the size of pheasants, and when they flew they showed beautiful white bands on their wings. These are the rare birds that have feathered feet and turn white in winter. They did not fly far, and several were so tame they did not fly at all. We got our little .22 revolvers and began to shoot at the nearest bird. He was some thirty feet distant. But we could not hit him, and at last Fox, getting disgusted, tried to catch the bird and made him fly. I felt relieved, for as we were getting closer and closer with every shot, it seemed possible that if the ptarmigan sat there long enough we might eventually have hit him. The mystery was why we shot so poorly. But this was explained by R. C., who discovered we had been shooting the wrong shells.

It was a long hard ride down the rough winding trail. But riding down was a vastly different thing from going up.

On September third we were up at five-thirty. It was clear and cold and the red of sunrise tinged the peaks. The snow banks looked pink. All the early morning scene was green, fresh, cool, with that mountain rareness of atmosphere.

We packed to break camp, and after breakfast it took hours to get our outfit in shape to start—a long string, resembling a caravan. I knew that events would occur that day. First we lost one of the dogs. Vern went back after him. The dogs were mostly chained in pairs, to prevent their running off. Sampson, the giant hound, was chained to a little dog, and the others were paired not according to size by any means. The poor dogs were disgusted with the arrangement. It developed presently that Cain, the bloodhound, a strange and wild hound much like Don of my old lion-hunting days, slipped us, and was not missed for hours. Teague decided to send back for him later.

Next in order of events, as we rode up the winding trail through the spruce forest, we met Teague's cow and calf, which he had kept all summer in camp. For some reason neither could be left. Teague told us to ride on, and an hour later when we halted to rest on the Flattop Mountain he came along with the rest of the train, and in the fore was the cow alone. It was evident that she was distressed and angry, for it took two men to keep her in the trail. And another thing plain to me was the fact that she was going to demoralize the pack horses. We were not across the wide range of this flat mountain when one of the pack animals, a lean and lanky sorrel, appeared suddenly to go mad, and began to buck off a pack. He succeeded. This inspired a black horse, very appropriately christened Nigger, to try his luck, and he shifted his pack in short order. It took patience, time, and effort to repack. The cow was a disorganizer. She took up as wide a trail as a road. And the pack animals, some with dignity and others with disgust, tried to avoid her vicinity. Going down the steep forest trail on the other side the real trouble began. The pack train split, ran and bolted, crashing through the trees, plunging down steep places, and jumping logs. It was a wild sort of chase. But luckily the packs remained intact until we were once more on open, flat ground. All went well for a while, except for an accident for which I was to blame. I spurred my horse, and he plunged suddenly past R. C.'s mount, colliding with him, tearing off my stirrup, and spraining R. C.'s ankle. This was almost a serious accident, as R. C. has an old baseball ankle that required favoring.

Next in order was the sorrel. As I saw it, he heedlessly went too near the cow, which we now called Bossy, and she acted somewhat like a Spanish Bull, to the effect that the sorrel was scared and angered at once. He began to run and plunge and buck right into the other pack animals, dropping articles from his pack as he dashed along. He stampeded the train, and gave the saddle horses a scare. When order was restored and the whole outfit gathered together again a full hour had been lost. By this time all the horses were tired, and that facilitated progress, because there were no more serious breaks.

Down in the valley it was hot, and the ride grew long and wearisome. Nevertheless, the scenery was beautiful. The valley was green and level, and a meandering stream formed many little lakes. On one side was a steep hill of sage and aspens, and on the other a black, spear-pointed spruce forest, rising sheer to a bold, blunt peak patched with snowbanks, and bronze and gray in the clear light. Huge white clouds sailed aloft, making dark moving shadows along the great slopes.

We reached our turning-off place about five o'clock, and again entered the fragrant, quiet forest—a welcome change. We climbed and climbed, at length coming into an open park of slopes and green borders of forest, with a lake in the center. We pitched camp on the skirt of the western slope, under the spruces, and worked hard to get the tents up and boughs cut for beds. Darkness caught us with our hands still full, and we ate supper in the light of a camp-fire, with the black, deep forest behind, and the pale afterglow across the lake.

I had a bad night, being too tired to sleep well. Many times I saw the moon shadows of spruce branches trembling on the tent walls, and the flickering shadows of the dying camp-fire. I heard the melodious tinkle of the bells on the hobbled horses. Bossy bawled often—a discordant break in the serenity of the night. Occasionally the hounds bayed her.

Toward morning I slept some, and awakened with what seemed a broken back. All, except R. C., were slow in crawling out. The sun rose hot. This lower altitude was appreciated by all. After breakfast we set to work to put the camp in order.

That afternoon we rode off to look over the ground. We crossed the park and worked up a timbered ridge remarkable for mossy, bare ground, and higher up for its almost total absence of grass or flowers. On the other side of this we had a fine view of Mt. Dome, a high peak across a valley. Then we worked down into the valley, which was full of parks and ponds and running streams. We found some fresh sign of deer, and a good deal of old elk and deer sign. But we saw no game of any kind. It was a tedious ride back through thick forest, where I observed many trees that had been barked by porcupines. Some patches were four feet from the ground, indicating that the porcupine had sat on the snow when he gnawed those particular places.

After sunset R. C. and I went off down a trail into the woods, and sitting down under a huge spruce we listened. The forest was solemn and still. Far down somewhere roared a stream, and that was all the sound we heard. The gray shadows darkened and gloom penetrated the aisles of the forest, until all the sheltered places were black as pitch. The spruces looked spectral—and speaking. The silence of the woods was deep, profound, and primeval. It all worked on my imagination until I began to hear faint sounds, and finally grand orchestral crashings of melody.

On our return the strange creeping chill, that must be a descendant of the old elemental fear, caught me at all obscure curves in the trail.

Next day we started off early, and climbed through the woods and into the parks under the Dome. We scared a deer that had evidently been drinking. His fresh tracks led before us, but we could not catch a glimpse of him.

We climbed out of the parks, up onto the rocky ridges where the spruce grew scarce, and then farther to the jumble of stones that had weathered from the great peaks above, and beyond that up the slope where all the vegetation was dwarfed, deformed, and weird, strange manifestation of its struggle for life.

Here the air grew keener and cooler, and the light seemed to expand. We rode on to the steep slope that led up to the gap we were to cross between the Dome and its companion.

I saw a red fox running up the slope, and dismounting I took a quick shot at three hundred yards, and scored a hit. It turned out to be a cross fox, and had very pretty fur.

When we reached the level of the deep gap the wind struck us hard and cold. On that side opened an abyss, gray and shelving as it led down to green timber, and then on to the yellow parks and black ridges that gleamed under the opposite range.

We had to work round a wide amphitheater, and up a steep corner to the top. This turned out to be level and smooth for a long way, with a short, velvety yellow grass, like moss, spotted with flowers. Here at thirteen thousand feet, the wind hit us with exceeding force, and soon had us with freezing hands and faces. All about us were bold black and gray peaks, with patches of snow, and above them clouds of white and drab, showing blue sky between. It developed that this grassy summit ascended in a long gradual sweep, from the apex of which stretched a grand expanse, like a plain of gold, down and down, endlessly almost, and then up and up to end under a gray butte, highest of the points around. The ride across here seemed to have no limit, but it was beautiful, though severe on endurance. I saw another fox, and dismounting, fired five shots as he ran, dusting him with three bullets. We rode out to the edge of the mountain and looked off. It was fearful, yet sublime. The world lay beneath us. In many places we rode along the rim, and at last

circled the great butte, and worked up behind it on a
swell of slope. Here the range ran west and the drop
was not sheer, but gradual with fine benches for
sheep. We found many tracks and fresh sign, but did
not see one sheep. Meanwhile the hard wind had
ceased, and the sun had come out, making the ride
comfortable, as far as weather was concerned. We
had gotten a long way from camp, and finding no
trail to descend in that direction we turned to retrace
our steps. That was about one o'clock, and we rode
and rode and rode, until I was so tired that I could
not appreciate the scenes as I had on the way up. It
took six hours to get back to camp!

Next morning we took the hounds and rode off for
bear. Eight of the hounds were chained in braces,
one big and one little dog together, and they certainly had a hard time of it. Sampson, the giant gray
and brown hound, and Jim, the old black leader,
were free to run to and fro across the way. We rode
down a few miles, and into the forest. There were
two long, black ridges, and here we were to hunt for
bear. It was the hardest kind of work, turning and
twisting between the trees, dodging snags, and brushing aside branches, and guiding a horse among fallen
logs. The forest was thick, and the ground was a rich
brown and black muck, soft to the horses' feet.
Many times the hounds got caught on snags, and had
to be released. Once Sampson picked up a scent of
some kind, and went off baying. Old Jim ran across
that trail and returned, thus making it clear that there
was no bear trail. We penetrated deep between the
two ridges, and came to a little lake, about thirty feet
wide, surrounded by rushes and grass. Here we rested
the horses, and incidentally, ourselves. Fox chased a

duck, and it flew into the woods and hid under a log. Fox trailed it, and Teague shot it just as he might have a rabbit. We got two more ducks, fine big mallards, the same way. It was amazing to me, and R. C. remarked that never had he seen such strange and foolish ducks.

This forest had hundreds of trees barked by porcupines, and some clear to the top. But we met only one of the animals, and he left several quills in the nose of one of the pups. I was of the opinion that these porcupines destroy many fine trees, as I saw a number barked all around.

We did not see any bear sign. On the way back to camp we rode out of the forest and down a wide valley, the opposite side of which was open slope with patches of alder. Even at a distance I could discern the color of these open glades and grassy benches. They had a tinge of purple, like purple sage. When I got to them I found a profusion of asters of the most exquisite shades of lavender, pink and purple. That slope was long, and all the way up we rode through these beautiful wild flowers. I shall never forget that sight, nor the many asters that shone like stars out of the green. The pink ones were new to me, and actually did not seem real. I noticed my horse occasionally nipped a bunch and ate them, which seemed to me almost as heartless as to tread them under foot.

When we got up the slope and into the woods again we met a storm, and traveled for an hour in the rain, and under the dripping spruces, feeling the cold wet sting of swaying branches as we rode by. Then the sun came out bright and the forest glittered, all gold and green. The smell of the woods after a rain is indescribable. It combines a rare tang of pine, spruce, earth and air, all refreshed.

The day after, we left at eight o'clock, and rode down to the main trail, and up that for five miles where we cut off to the left and climbed into the timber. The woods were fresh and dewy, dark and cool, and for a long time we climbed bench after bench where the grass and ferns and moss made a thick, deep cover. Farther up we got into fallen timber and made slow progress. At timber line we tied the horses and climbed up to the pass between two great mountain ramparts. Sheep tracks were in evidence, but not very fresh. Teague and I climbed on top and R. C., with Vern, went below just along the timber line. The climb on foot took all my strength, and many times I had to halt for breath. The air was cold. We stole along the rim and peered over. R. C. and Vern looked like very little men far below, and the dogs resembled mice.

Teague climbed higher, and left me on a promontory, watching all around.

The cloud pageant was magnificent, with huge billowy white masses across the valley, and to the west great black thunderheads rolling up. The wind began to blow hard, carrying drops of rain that stung, and the air was nipping cold. I felt aloof from all the crowded world, alone on the windy heights, with clouds and storm all around me.

When the storm threatened I went back to the horses. It broke, but was not severe after all. At length R. C. and the men returned and we mounted to ride back to camp. The storm blew away, leaving the sky clear and blue, and the sun shone warm. We had an hour of winding in and out among windfalls of timber, and jumping logs, and breaking through brush. Then the way sloped down to a beautiful forest, shady and green, full of mossy dells, almost overgrown with ferns and low spreading ground pine or spruce. The aisles of the forest were long and shaded by the stately spruces. Water ran through every ravine, sometimes a brawling brook, sometimes a rivulet hidden under overhanging mossy banks. We scared up two lonely grouse, at long intervals. At length we got into fallen timber, and from that worked into a jumble of rocks, where the going was rough and dangerous.

The afternoon waned as we rode on and on, up and down, in and out, around, and at times the horses stood almost on their heads, sliding down steep places where the earth was soft and black, and gave forth a dank odor. We passed ponds and swamps, and little lakes. We saw where beavers had gnawed down aspens, and we just escaped miring our horses in marshes, where the grass grew, rich and golden, hiding the treacherous mire. The sun set, and still we did not seem to get anywhere. I was afraid darkness would overtake us, and we would get lost in the woods. Presently we struck an old elk trail, and following that for a while, came to a point where R. C. and I recognized a tree and a glade where we had been before—and not far from camp—a welcome discovery.

Next day we broke camp and started across country for new territory near Whitley's Peak.

We rode east up the mountain. After several miles along an old logging road we reached the timber, and eventually the top of the ridge. We went down, crossing parks and swales. There were cattle pas-

tures, and eaten over and trodden so much they had
no beauty left. Teague wanted to camp at a salt lick,
but I did not care for the place.

We went on. The dogs crossed a bear trail, and
burst out in a clamor. We had a hard time holding
them.

The guide and I had a hot argument. I did not
want to stay there and chase a bear in a cow pasture. . . . So we went on, down into ranch country,
and this disgusted me further. We crossed a ranch,
and rode several miles on a highway, then turned
abruptly, and climbed a rough, rocky ridge, covered
with brush and aspen. We crossed it, and went down
for several miles, and had to camp in an aspen
grove, on the slope of a ravine. It was an uninviting
place to stay, but as there was no other we had to
make the best of it. The afternoon had waned. I took
a gun and went off down the ravine, until I came to
a deep gorge. Here I heard the sound of a brawling
brook. I sat down for an hour, but saw no game.

That night I had a wretched bed, one that I could
hardly stay in, and I passed miserable hours. I got up
sore, cramped, sleepy and irritable. We had to wait
three hours for the horses to be caught and packed. I
had predicted straying horses. At last we were off,
and rode along the steep slope of a canyon for
several miles, and then struck a stream of amber-
colored water. As we climbed along this we came
into deep spruce forest, where it was pleasure to
ride. I saw many dells and nooks, cool and shady,
full of mossy rocks and great trees. But flowers were
scarce. We were sorry to pass the head-springs of
that stream and to go on over the divide and down
into the wooded, but dry and stony country. We rode

until late, and came at last to a park where sheep had been run. I refused to camp here, and Teague, in high dudgeon, rode on. As it turned out I was both wise and lucky, for we rode into a park with many branches, where there was good water and fair grass and a pretty grove of white pines in which to pitch our tents. I enjoyed this camp, and had a fine rest at night.

The morning broke dark and lowering. We hustled to get started before a storm broke. It began to rain as we mounted our horses, and soon we were in the midst of a cold rain. It blew hard. We put on our slickers. After a short ride down through the forest we entered Buffalo Park. This was a large park, and we lost time trying to find a forester's trail leading out of it. At last we found one, but it soon petered out, and we were lost in thick timber, in a driving rain, with the cold and wind increasing. But we kept on.

This forest was deep and dark, with tremendous windfalls, and great canyons around which we had to travel. It took us hours to ride out of it. When we began to descend once more we struck an old lumber road. More luck—the storm ceased, and presently we were out on an aspen slope with a great valley beneath, and high, black peaks beyond. Below the aspens were long swelling slopes of sage and grass, gray and golden and green. A ranch lay in the valley, and we crossed it to climb up a winding ravine, once more to the aspens where we camped in the rancher's pasture. It was a cold, wet camp, but we managed to be fairly comfortable.

The sunset was gorgeous. The mass of clouds broke and rolled. There was exquisite golden light on the peaks, and many rose- and violet-hued banks of cloud.

Morning found us shrouded in fog. We were late starting. About nine the curtain of gray began to lift and break. We climbed pastures and aspen thickets, high up to the spruce, where the grass grew luxuriant, and the red wall of rock overhung the long slopes. The view west was magnificent—a long, bulging range of mountains, vast stretches of green aspen slopes, winding parks of all shapes, gray and gold and green, and jutting peaks, and here and there patches of autumn blaze in grass and thicket.

We spent the afternoon pitching camp on an aspen knoll, with water, grass, and wood near at hand, and the splendid view of mountains and valleys below.

We spent many full days under the shadow of Whitley's Peak. After the middle of September the aspens colored and blazed to the touch of frost, and the mountain slopes were exceedingly beautiful. Against a background of gray sage the gold and red and purple aspen groves showed too much like exquisite paintings to seem real. In the mornings the frost glistened thick and white on the grass; and after the gorgeous sunsets of gold over the violet-hazed ranges the air grew stingingly cold.

Bear-chasing with a pack of hounds has been severely criticized by many writers and I was among them. I believed it a cowardly business, and that was why, if I chased bears with dogs, I wanted to chase the kind that could not be treed. But like many another I did not know what I was writing about. I did not shoot a bear out of a tree and I would not do so, except in a case of hunger. All the same, leaving the tree out of consideration, bear-chasing with hounds is a tremendously exciting and hazardous game. But my ideas about sport are changing. Hunting, in the sportsman's sense, is a cruel and degenerate business.

The more I hunt the more I become convinced of something wrong about the game. I am a different man when I get a gun in my hands. All is exciting, hotpressed, red. Hunting is magnificent up to the moment the shot is fired. After that it is another matter. It is useless for sportsmen to tell me that they, in particular, hunt right, conserve the game, do not go beyond the limit, and all that sort of thing. I do not believe them and I never met the guide who did. A rifle is made for killing. When a man goes out with one he means to kill. He may keep within the law, but that is not the question. It is a question of spirit, and men who love to hunt are yielding to and always developing the old primitive instinct to kill. The meaning of the spirit of life is not clear to them. An argument may be advanced that, according to the laws of self-preservation and the survival of the fittest, if a man stops all strife, all fight, then he will retrograde. And that is to say if a man does not go to the wilds now and then, and work hard and live some semblance of the life of his progenitors, he will weaken. It seems that he will, but I am not prepared now to say whether or not that would be well. The Germans believe they are the race fittest to survive over all others—and that has made me a little sick of this Darwin business.

To return, however, to the fact that to ride after hounds on a wild chase is a dangerous and wonderfully exhilarating experience, I will relate a couple of instances, and I will leave it to my readers to judge whether or not it is a cowardly sport.

One afternoon a rancher visited our camp and informed us that he had surprised a big black bear eating the carcass of a dead cow.

"Good! We'll have a bear to-morrow night," declared Teague, in delight. "We'll get him even if the trail is a day old. But he'll come back to-night."

Early next morning the young rancher and three other boys rode into camp, saying they would like to go with us to see the fun. We were glad to have them, and we rode off through the frosted sage that crackled like brittle glass under the hoofs of the horses. Our guide led toward a branch of a park, and when we got within perhaps a quarter of a mile Teague suggested that R. C. and I go ahead on the chance of surprising the bear. It was owing to this suggestion that my brother and I were well ahead of the others. But we did not see any bear near the carcass of the cow. Old Jim and Sampson were close behind us, and when Jim came within forty yards of that carcass he put his nose up with a deep and ringing bay, and he shot by us like a streak. He never went near the dead cow! Sampson bayed like thunder and raced after Jim.

"They're off!" I yelled to R. C. "It's a hot scent! Come on!"

We spurred our horses and they broke across the open park to the edge of the woods. Jim and Sampson were running straight with noses high. I heard a string of yelps and bellows from our rear.

"Look back!" shouted R. C.

Teague and the cowboys were unleashing the rest of the pack. It surely was great to see them stretch out, yelping wildly. Like the wind they passed us. Jim and Sampson headed into the woods with deep

bays. I was riding Teague's best horse for this sort
of work and he understood the game and plainly
enjoyed it. R. C.'s horse ran as fast in the woods as
he did in the open. This frightened me, and I yelled
to R. C. to be careful. I yelled to deaf ears. That is
the first great risk—a rider is not going to be careful!
We were right on top of Jim and Sampson with the
pack clamoring mad music just behind. The forest
rang. Both horses hurdled logs, sometimes two at
once. My old lion chases with Buffalo Jones had
made me skillful in dodging branches and snags, and
sliding knees back to avoid knocking them against
trees. For a mile the forest was comparatively open,
and here we had a grand and ringing run. I received
two hard knocks, was unseated once, but held on,
and I got a stinging crack in the face from a branch.
R. C. added several more black-and-blue spots to his
already spotted anatomy, and he missed, just by an
inch, a solid snag that would have broken him in
two. The pack stretched out in wild staccato chorus,
the little Airedales literally screeching. Jim got out
of our sight and then Sampson. Still it was ever
more thrilling to follow by sound rather than sight.
They led up a thick, steep slope. Here we got into
trouble in the windfalls of timber and the pack drew
away from us, up over the mountain. We were half
way up when we heard them jump the bear. The
forest seemed full of strife and bays and yelps. We
heard the dogs go down again to our right, and as we
turned we saw Teague and the others strung out
along the edge of the park. They got far ahead of us.
When we reached the bottom of the slope they were
out of sight, but we could hear them yell. The
hounds were working around on another slope, from

which craggy rocks loomed above the timber. R. C.'s
horse lunged across the park and appeared to be
running off from mine. I was a little to the right, and
when my horse got under way, full speed, we had
the bad luck to plunge suddenly into soft ground. He
went to his knees, and I sailed out of the saddle fully
twenty feet, to alight all spread out and to slide like
a plow. I did not seem to be hurt. When I got up my
horse was coming and he appeared to be patient with
me, but he was in a hurry. Before we got across the
wet place R. C. was out of sight. I decided that
instead of worrying about him I had better think
about myself. Once on hard ground my horse fairly
charged into the woods and we broke brush and
branches as if they had been punk. It was again open
forest, then a rocky slope, and then a flat ridge with
aisles between the trees. Here I heard the melodious
notes of Teague's hunting horn, and following that,
the full chorus of the hounds. They had treed the
bear. Coming into still more open forest, with rocks
here and there, I caught sight of R. C. far ahead, and
soon I had glimpses of the other horses, and lastly,
while riding full tilt, I spied a big, black, glistening
bear high up in a pine a hundred yards or more
distant.

Slowing down I rode up to the circle of frenzied
dogs and excited men. The boys were all jabbering
at once. Teague was beaming. R. C. sat his horse,
and it struck me that he looked sorry for the bear.

"Fifteen minutes!" ejaculated Teague, with a proud
glance at Old Jim standing with forepaws up on the
pine.

Indeed it had been a short and ringing chase.

All the time while I fooled around trying to photo-

graph the treed bear, R. C. sat there on his horse,
looking upward.

"Well, gentlemen, better kill him," said Teague,
cheerfully. "If he gets rested he'll come down."

It was then I suggested to R. C. that he do the
shooting.

"Not much!" he exclaimed.

The bear looked really pretty perched up there. He
was as round as a barrel and black as jet and his fur
shone in the gleams of sunlight. His tongue hung
out, and his plump sides heaved, showing what a
quick, hard run he had made before being driven to
the tree. What struck me most forcibly about him
was the expression in his eyes as he looked down at
those devils of hounds. He was scared. He realized
his peril. It was utterly impossible for me to see
Teague's point of view.

"Go ahead—and plug him," I replied to my
brother. "Get it over."

"You do it," he said.

"No, I won't."

"Why not—I'd like to know?"

"Maybe we won't have so good a chance again—
and I want you to get your bear," I replied.

"Why it's like—murder," he protested.

"Oh, not so bad as that," I returned, weakly.
"We need the meat. We've not had any game meat,
you know, except ducks and grouse."

"You won't do it?" he added, grimly.

"No, I refuse."

Meanwhile the young ranchers gazed at us with
wide eyes and the expression on Teague's honest,
ruddy face would have been funny under other
circumstances.

"That bear will come down an' mebbe kill one of my dogs," he protested.

"Well, he can come for all I care," I replied, positively, and I turned away.

I heard R. C. curse low under his breath. Then followed the spang of his .35 Remington. I wheeled in time to see the bear straining upward in terrible convulsion, his head pointed high, with blood spurting from his nose. Slowly he swayed and fell with a heavy crash.

The next bear chase we had was entirely different medicine.

Off in the basin under the White Slides, back of our camp, the hounds struck a fresh track and in an instant were out of sight. With the cowboy Vern setting the pace we plunged after them. It was rough country. Bogs, brooks, swales, rocky little parks, stretches of timber full of windfalls, groves of aspens so thick we could scarcely squeeze through—all these obstacles soon allowed the hounds to get far away. We came out into a large park, right under the mountain slope, and here we sat our horses listening to the chase. That trail led around the basin and back near to us, up the thick green slope, where high up near a ledge we heard the pack jump this bear. It sounded to us as if he had been roused out of a sleep.

"I'll bet it's one of the big grizzlies we've heard about," said Teague.

That was something to my taste. I have seen a few grizzlies. Riding to higher ground I kept close watch on the few open patches up on the slope. The chase led toward us for a while. Suddenly I saw a big bear with a frosted coat go lumbering across one of these openings.

"Silvertip! Silvertip!" I yelled at the top of my lungs. "I saw him!"

My call thrilled everybody. Vern spurred his horse and took to the right. Teague advised that we climb the slope. So we made for the timber. Once there we had to get off and climb on foot. It was steep, rough, very hard work. I had on chaps and spurs. Soon I was hot, laboring, and my heart began to hurt. We all had to rest. The baying of the hounds inspirited us now and then, but presently we lost it. Teague said they had gone over the ridge and as soon as we got up to the top we would hear them again. We struck an elk trail with fresh elk tracks in it. Teague said they were just ahead of us. I never climbed so hard and fast in my life. We were all tuckered out when we reached the top of the ridge. Then to our great disappointment we did not hear the hounds. Mounting we rode along the crest of this wooded ridge toward the western end, which was considerably higher. Once on a bare patch of ground we saw where the grizzly had passed. The big, round tracks, toeing in a little, made a chill go over me. No doubt of its being a silvertip!

We climbed and rode to the high point, and coming out upon the summit of the mountain we all heard the deep, hoarse baying of the pack. They were in the canyon down a bare grassy slope and over a wooded bench at our feet. Teague yelled as he spurred down. R. C. rode hard in his tracks.

But my horse was new to this bear chasing. He was mettlesome, and he did not want to do what I wanted. When I jabbed the spurs into his flanks he

nearly bucked me off. I was looking for a soft place
to light when he quit. Long before I got down that
open slope Teague and R. C. had disappeared. I had
to follow their tracks. This I did at a gallop, but now
and then lost the tracks, and had to haul in to find
them. If I could have heard the hounds from there I
would have gone on anyway. But once down in the
jack-pines I could hear neither yell or bay. The pines
were small, close together, and tough. I hurt my
hands, scratched my face, barked my knees. The
horse had a habit of suddenly deciding to go the way
he liked instead of the way I guided him, and when
he plunged between saplings too close together to
permit us both to go through, it was exceedingly
hard on me. I was worked into a frenzy. Suppose R. C.
should come face to face with that old grizzly and
fail to kill him! That was the reason for my desperate
hurry. I got a crack on the head that nearly blinded
me. My horse grew hot and began to run in every
little open space. He could scarcely be held in. And
I, with the blood hot in me too, did not hold him
hard enough.

It seemed miles across that wooded bench. But at
last I reached another slope. Coming out upon a
canyon rim I heard R. C. and Teague yelling, and I
heard the hounds fighting the grizzly. He was growling and threshing about far below. I had missed the
tracks made by Teague and my brother, and it was
necessary to find them. That slope looked impassable. I rode back along the rim, then forward. Finally I found where the ground was plowed deep and
here I headed my horse. He had been used to smooth
roads and he could not take these jumps. I went
forward on his neck. But I hung on and spurred him

hard. The mad spirit of that chase had gotten into him too. All the time I could hear the fierce baying and yelping of the hounds, and occasionally I heard a savage bawl from the bear. I literally plunged, slid, broke a way down that mountain slope, riding all the time, before I discovered the footprints of Teague and R. C. They had walked, leading their horses. By this time I was so mad I would not get off. I rode all the way down that steep slope of dense saplings, loose rock slides and earth, and jumble of splintered cliff. That he did not break my neck and his own spoke the truth about that roan horse. Despite his inexperience he was great. We fell over one bank, but a thicket of aspens saved us from rolling. The avalanches slid from under us until I imagined that the grizzly would be scared. Once as I stopped to listen I heard bear and pack farther down the canyon—heard them above the roar of a rushing stream. They went on and I lost the sounds of fight. But R. C.'s clear thrilling call floated up to me. Probably he was worried about me.

Then before I realized it I was at the foot of the slope, in a narrow canyon bed, full of rocks and trees, with the din of roaring water in my ears. I could hear nothing else. Tracks were everywhere, and when I came to the first open place I was thrilled. The grizzly had plunged off a sandy bar into the water, and there he had fought the hounds. Signs of that battle were easy to read. I saw where his huge tracks, still wet, led up the opposite sandy bank.

Then, down stream, I did my most reckless riding. On level ground the horse was splendid. Once he leaped clear across the brook. Every plunge, every turn I expected to bring me upon my brother and Teague and that fighting pack. More than once I thought I heard the spang of the .35 and this made me urge the roan faster and faster.

The canyon narrowed, the stream-bed deepened. I had to slow down to get through the trees and rocks. And suddenly I was overjoyed to ride pell-mell upon R. C. and Teague with half the panting hounds. The canyon had grown too rough for the horses to go farther and it would have been useless for us to try on foot. As I dismounted, so sore and bruised I could hardly stand, old Jim came limping in to fall into the brook where he lapped and lapped thirstily. Teague threw up his hands. Old Jim's return meant an ended chase. The grizzly had eluded the hounds in that jumble of rocks below.

"Say, did you meet the bear?" queried Teague, eyeing me in astonishment and mirth.

Bloody, dirty, ragged and wringing wet with sweat I must have been a sight. R. C. however, did not look so very immaculate, and when I saw he also was lame and scratched and black I felt better.

CHAPTER THREE

Roping Lions in the Grand Canyon

I

The Grand Canyon of Arizona is over two hundred
miles long, thirteen wide, and a mile and a half
deep; a titanic gorge in which mountains, tablelands,
chasms and cliffs lie half veiled in purple haze. It is
wild and sublime, a thing of wonder, of mystery;
beyond all else a place to grip the heart of a man, to
unleash his daring spirit.

On April 20th, 1908, after days on the hot desert,
my weary party and pack train reached the summit
of Powell's Plateau, the most isolated, inaccessible
and remarkable mesa of any size in all the canyon
country. Cut off from the mainland it appeared insurmountable; standing aloof from the towers and
escarpments, rugged and bold in outline, its forest
covering like a strip of black velvet, its giant granite
walls gold in the sun, it seemed apart from the
world, haunting with its beauty, isolation and wild
promise.

The members of my party harmoniously fitted the
scene. Buffalo Jones, burly-shouldered, bronze-faced,

and grim, proved in his appearance what a lifetime on the plains could make of a man. Emett was a Mormon, a massively built grey-bearded son of the desert; he had lived his life on it; he had conquered it and in his falcon eyes shone all its fire and freedom. Ranger Jim Owens had the wiry, supple body and careless, tidy garb of the cowboy, and the watchful gaze, quiet face and locked lips of the frontiersman. The fourth member was a Navajo Indian, a copper-skinned, raven-haired, beady-eyed desert savage.

I had told Emett to hire some one who could put the horses on grass in the evening and then find them the next morning. In northern Arizona this required more than genius. Emett secured the best trailer of the desert Navajos. Jones hated an Indian; and Jim, who carried an ounce of lead somewhere in his person, associated this painful addition to his weight with an unfriendly Apache, and swore all Indians should be dead. So between the two, Emett and I had trouble in keeping our Navajo from illustrating the plainsman idea of a really good Indian—a dead one.

While we were pitching camp among magnificent pine trees, and above a hollow where a heavy bank of snow still lay, a sodden pounding in the turf attracted our attention.

"Hold the horses!" yelled Emett.

As we all made a dive among our snorting and plunging horses the sound seemed to be coming right into camp. In a moment I saw a string of wild horses thundering by. A noble black stallion led them, and as he ran with beautiful stride he curved his fine head backward to look at us, and whistled his wild challenge.

Later a herd of large white-tailed deer trooped up the hollow. The Navajo grew much excited and wanted me to shoot, and when Emett told him we had not come out to kill, he looked dumbfounded. Even the Indian felt it a strange departure from the usual mode of hunting to travel and climb hundreds of miles over hot desert and rock-ribbed canyons, to camp at last in a spot so wild that deer were tame as cattle, and then not kill.

Nothing could have pleased me better, incident to the settling into permanent camp. The wild horses and tame deer added the all-satisfying touch to the background of forest, flowers and mighty pines and sunlit patches of grass, the white tents and red blankets, the sleeping hounds and blazing fire-logs all making a picture like that of a hunter's dream.

"Come, saddle up," called the never restful Jones. "Leave the Indian in camp with the hounds, and we'll get the lay of the land." All afternoon we spent riding the plateau. What a wonderful place! We were completely bewildered with its physical properties, and surprised at the abundance of wild horses and mustangs, deer, coyotes, foxes, grouse and other birds, and overjoyed to find innumerable lion trails. When we returned to camp I drew a rough map, which Jones laid flat on the ground as he called us around him.

"Now, boys, let's get our heads together."

In shape the plateau resembled the ace of clubs. The center and side wings were high and well wooded with heavy pines; the middle wing was longest, sloped west, had no pine, but a dense growth of cedar. Numerous ridges and canyons cut up this central wing. Middle Canyon, the longest and deepest, bisected the plateau, headed near camp, and ran parallel with two smaller ones, which we named Right and Left Canyons. These three were lion runways and hundreds of deer carcasses lined the thickets. North Hollow was the only depression, as well as runway, on the northwest rim. West Point formed the extreme western cape of the plateau. To the left of West Point was a deep cut-in of the rim wall, called the Bay. The three important canyons opened into it. From the Bay, the south rim was regular and impassable all the way round to the narrow Saddle, which connected it to the mainland.

"Now then," said Jones, when we assured him that we were pretty well informed as to the important features, "you can readily see our advantage. The plateau is about nine or ten miles long, and six wide at its widest. We can't get lost, at least for long. We know where lions can go over the rim and we'll head them off, make short cut chases, something new in lion hunting. We are positive the lions can not get over the second wall, except where we came up, at the Saddle. In regard to lion signs, I'm doubtful of the evidence of my own eyes. This is virgin ground. No white man or Indian has ever hunted lions here. We have stumbled on a lion home, the breeding place of hundreds of lions that infest the north rim of the canyon."

The old plainsman struck a big fist into the palm of his hand, a rare action with him. Jim lifted his broad hat and ran his fingers through his white hair. In Emett's clear desert-eagle eyes shown a furtive, anxious look, which yet could not overshadow the smouldering fire.

"If only we don't kill the horses!" he said.

More than anything else that remark from such a man thrilled me with its subtle suggestion. He loved those beautiful horses. What wild rides he saw in his mind's eye! In cold calculation we perceived the wonderful possibilities never before experienced by hunters, and as the wild spell clutched us my last bar of restraint let down.

During supper we talked incessantly, and afterward around the camp-fire. Twilight fell with the dark shadows sweeping under the silent pines; the night wind rose and began its moan.

"Shore there's some scent on the wind," said Jim, lighting his pipe with a red ember. "See how oneasy Don is."

The hound raised his fine, dark head and repeatedly sniffed the air, then walked to and fro as if on guard for his pack. Moze ground his teeth on a bone and growled at one of the pups. Sounder was sleepy, but he watched Don with suspicious eyes. The other hounds, mature and somber, lay stretched before the fire.

"Tie them up, Jim," said Jones, "and let's turn in."

II

When I awakened next morning the sound of Emett's axe rang out sharply. Little streaks of light from the camp-fire played between the flaps of the tent. I saw old Moze get up and stretch himself. A jangle of cowbells from the forest told me we would not have to wait for the horses that morning.

"The Injun's all right," Jones remarked to Emett.

"All rustle for breakfast," called Jim.

We ate in the semi-darkness with the gray shadow ever brightening. Dawn broke as we saddled our horses. The pups were limber, and ran to and fro on their chains, scenting the air; the older hounds stood quietly waiting.

"Come Navvy—come chase cougie," said Emett.

"Dam! No!" replied the Indian.

"Let him keep camp," suggested Jim.

"All right; but he'll eat us out," Emett declared.

"Climb up you fellows," said Jones, impatiently. "Have I got everything—rope, chains, collars, wire, nippers? Yes, all right. Hyar, you lazy dogs—out of this!"

We rode abreast down the ridge. The demeanor of the hounds contrasted sharply with what it had been at the start of the hunt the year before. Then they had been eager, uncertain, violent; they did not know what was in the air; now they filed after Don in an orderly trot.

We struck out of the pines at half past five. Floating mist hid the lower end of the plateau. The morning had a cool touch but there was no frost. Crossing Middle Canyon about half way down we jogged on. Cedar trees began to show bright green against the soft gray sage. We were nearing the dark line of the cedar forest when Jim, who led, held up his hand in a warning check. We closed in around him.

"Watch Don," he said.

The hound stood stiff, head well up, nose working, and the hair on his back bristling. All the other hounds whined and kept close to him.

"Don scents a lion," whispered Jim. "I've never known him to do that unless there was the scent of a lion on the wind."

"Hunt 'em up Don, old boy," called Jones.

The pack commenced to work back and forth along the ridge. We neared a hollow when Don barked eagerly. Sounder answered and likewise Jude. Moze's short angry "bow-wow" showed the old gladiator to be in line.

"Ranger's gone," cried Jim. "He was farthest ahead. I'll bet he's struck it. We'll know in a minute, for we're close."

The hounds were tearing through the sage, working harder and harder, calling and answering one another, all the time getting down into the hollow.

Don suddenly let out a string of yelps. I saw him, running head up, pass into the cedars like a yellow dart. Sounder howled his deep, full bay, and led the rest of the pack up the slope in angry clamor.

"They're off!" yelled Jim, and so were we.

In less than a minute we had lost one another. Crashings among the dry cedars, thud of hoofs and yells kept me going in one direction. The fiery burst of the hounds had surprised me. I remembered that Jim had said Emett and his charger might keep the pack in sight, but that none of the rest of us could.

It did not take me long to realize what my mustang was made of. His name was Foxie, which suited him well. He carried me at a fast pace on the trail of some one; and he seemed to know that by keeping in this trail part of the work of breaking through the brush was already done for him. Nevertheless, the sharp dead branches, more numerous in a cedar forest than elsewhere, struck and stung us as we passed. We climbed a ridge, and found the cedars thinning out into open patches. Then we faced a bare slope of sage and I saw Emett below on his big horse.

Foxie bolted down this slope, hurdling the bunches of sage, and showing the speed of which Emett had boasted. The open ground, with its brush, rock and gullies, was easy going for the little mustang. I heard nothing save the wind singing in my ears. Emett's trail, plain in the yellow ground showed me the way. On entering the cedars again I pulled Foxie in and stopped twice to yell "waa-hoo!" I heard the baying of the hounds, but no answer to my signal. Then I attended to the stern business of catching up. For what seemed a long time, I threaded the maze of cedar, galloped the open sage flats, always on Emett's track.

A signal cry, sharp to the right, turned me. I answered, and with the exchange of signal cries found my way into an open glade where Jones and Jim awaited me.

"Here's one," said Jim. "Emett must be with the hounds. Listen."

With the labored breathing of the horses filling our ears we could hear no other sound. Dismounting, I went aside and turned my ear to the breeze.

"I hear Don," I cried instantly.

"Which way?" both men asked.

"West."

"Strange," said Jones. "The hound wouldn't split, would he, Jim?"

"Don leave that hot trail? Shore he wouldn't," replied Jim. "But his runnin' do seem queer this morning."

"The breeze is freshening," I said. "There! Now listen! Don, and Sounder, too."

The baying came closer and closer. Our horses threw up long ears. It was hard to sit still and wait. At a quick cry from Jim we saw Don cross the lower end of the flat.

No need to spur our mounts! The lifting of bridles served, and away we raced. Foxie passed the others in short order. Don had long disappeared, but with blended bays, Jude, Moze, and Sounder broke out of the cedars hot on the trail. They, too, were out of sight in a moment.

The crash of breaking brush and thunder of hoofs from where the hounds had come out of the forest, attracted and even frightened me. I saw the green of a low cedar tree shake, and split, to let out a huge, gaunt horse with a big man doubled over his saddle. The onslaught of Emett and his desert charger stirred a fear in me that checked admiration.

"Hounds running wild," he yelled, and the dark shadows of the cedars claimed him again.

A hundred yards within the forest we came again upon Emett, dismounted, searching the ground. Moze and Sounder were with him, apparently at fault. Suddenly Moze left the little glade and venting his sullen, quick bark, disappeared under the trees. Sounder sat on his haunches and yelped.

"Now what the hell is wrong?" growled Jones tumbling off his saddle.

"Shore something is," said Jim, also dismounting.

"Here's a lion track," interposed Emett.

"Ha! and here's another," cried Jones, in great satisfaction. "That's the trail we were on, and here's another crossing it at right angles. Both are fresh: one isn't fifteen minutes old. Don and Jude have split one way and Moze another. By George! that's great of Sounder to hang fire!''

''Put him on the fresh trail,'' said Jim, vaulting into his saddle.

Jones complied, with the result that we saw Sounder start off on the trail Moze had taken. All of us got in some pretty hard riding, and managed to stay within earshot of Sounder. We crossed a canyon, and presently reached another which, from its depth, must have been Middle Canyon. Sounder did not climb the opposite slope, so we followed the rim. From a bare ridge we distinguished the line of pines above us, and decided that our location was in about the center of the plateau.

Very little time elapsed before we heard Moze. Sounder had caught up with him. We came to a halt where the canyon widened and was not so deep, with cliffs and cedars opposite us, and an easy slope leading down. Sounder bayed incessantly; Moze emitted harsh, eager howls, and both hounds, in plain sight, began working in circles.

''The lion has gone up somewhere,'' cried Jim. ''Look sharp!''

Repeatedly Moze worked to the edge of a low wall of stone and looked over; then he barked and ran back to the slope, only to return. When I saw him slide down a steep place, make for the bottom of the stone wall, and jump into the low branches of a cedar I knew where to look. Then I descried the lion a round yellow ball, cunningly curled up in a mass of dark branches. He had leaped into the tree from the wall.

''There he is! Treed! Treed!'' I yelled. ''Moze has found him.''

"Down boys, down into the canyon," shouted Jones, in sharp voice. "Make a racket, we don't want him to jump."

How he and Jim and Emett rolled and cracked the stone! For a moment I could not get off my horse; I was chained to my saddle by a strange vacillation that could have been no other thing than fear.

"Are you afraid?" called Jones from below.

"Yes, but I am coming," I replied, and dismounted to plunge down the hill. It may have been shame or anger that dominated me then; whatever it was I made directly for the cedar, and did not halt until I was under the snarling lion.

"Not too close!" warned Jones. "He might jump. It's a Tom, a two-year-old, and full of fight."

It did not matter to me then whether he jumped or not. I knew I had to be cured of my dread, and the sooner it was done the better.

Old Moze had already climbed a third of the distance up to the lion.

"Hyar Moze! Out of there, you rascal coon chaser!" Jones yelled as he threw stones and sticks at the hound. Moze, however, replied with his snarly bark and climbed on steadily.

"I've got to pull him out. Watch close boys and tell me if the lion starts down."

When Jones climbed the first few branches of the tree, Tom let out an ominous growl.

"Make ready to jump. Shore he's comin'," called Jim.

The lion, snarling viciously, started to descend. It was a ticklish moment for all of us, particularly Jones. Warily he backed down.

"Boys, maybe he's bluffing," said Jones. "Try

him out. Grab sticks and run at the tree and yell, as
if you were going to kill him.''

Not improbably the demonstration we executed
under the tree would have frightened even an Afri-
can lion. Tom hesitated, showed his white fangs,
returned to his first perch, and from there climbed as
far as he could. The forked branch on which he
stood swayed alarmingly.

"Here, punch Moze out," said Jim handing up a
long pole.

The old hound hung like a leech to the tree,
making it difficult to dislodge him. At length he fell
heavily, and venting his thick battle cry, attempted
to climb again.

Jim seized him, made him fast to the rope with
which Sounder had already been tied.

"Say Emett, I've no chance here," called Jones.
"You try to throw at him from the rock."

Emett ran up the rock, coiled his lasso and cast
the noose. It sailed perfectly in between the branches
and circled Tom's head. Before it could be slipped
tight he had thrown it off. Then he hid behind the
branches.

"I'm going farther up," said Jones.

"Be quick," yelled Jim.

Jones evidently had that in mind. When he reached
the middle fork of the cedar, he stood erect and
extended the noose of his lasso on the point of his
pole. Tom, with a hiss and snap, struck at it savagely. The second trial tempted the lion to saw the
rope with his teeth. In a flash Jones withdrew the
pole, and lifted a loop of the slack rope over the
lion's ears.

"Pull!" he yelled.

Emett, at the other end of the lasso, threw his great strength into action, pulling the lion out with a crash, and giving the cedar such a tremendous shaking that Jones lost his footing and fell heavily.

Thrilling as the moment was, I had to laugh, for Jones came up out of a cloud of dust, as angry as a wet hornet, and made prodigious leaps to get out of the reach of the whirling lion.

"Look out!——!" he bawled.

Tom, certainly none the worse for his tumble, made three leaps, two at Jones, one at Jim, which was checked by the short length of the rope in Emett's hands. Then for a moment, a thick cloud of dust enveloped the wrestling lion, during which the quick-witted Jones tied the free end of the lasso to a sapling.

"Dod gast the luck!" yelled Jones reaching for another lasso. "I didn't mean for you to pull him out of the tree. Now he'll get loose or kill himself."

When the dust cleared away, we discovered our prize stretched out at full length and frothing at the mouth. As Jones approached, the lion began a series of evolutions so rapid as to be almost indiscernible to the eye. I saw a wheel of dust and yellow fur. Then came a thud and the lion lay inert.

Jones pounced upon him and loosed the lasso around his neck.

"I think he's done for, but maybe not. He's breathing yet. Here, help me tie his paws together. Look out! He's coming to!"

The lion stirred and raised his head. Jones ran the loop of the second lasso around the two hind paws and stretched the lion out. While in this helpless position and with no strength and hardly any breath left in him the lion was easy to handle. With Emett's help Jones quickly clipped the sharp claws, tied the four paws together, took off the neck lasso and substituted a collar and chain.

"There, that's one. He'll come to all right," said Jones. "But we are lucky. Emett, never pull another lion clear out of a tree. Pull him over a limb and hang him there while some one below ropes his hind paws. That's the only way, and if we don't stick to it, somebody is going to get done for. Come, now, we'll leave this fellow here and hunt up Don and Jude. They've treed another lion by this time."

Remarkable to me was to see how, as soon as the lion lay helpless, Sounder lost his interest. Moze growled, yet readily left the spot. Before we reached the level, both hounds had disappeared.

"Hear that?" yelled Jones, digging spurs into his horse. "Hi! Hi! Hi!"

From the cedars rang the thrilling, blending chorus of bays that told of a treed lion. The forest was almost impenetrable. We had to pick our way. Emett forged ahead; we heard him smashing the deadwood; and soon a yell proclaimed the truth of Jones' assertion.

First I saw the men looking upward; then Moze climbing the cedar, and the other hounds with noses skyward; and last, in the dead top of the tree, a dark blot against the blue, a big tawny lion.

"Whoop!" The yell leaped past my lips. Quiet Jim was yelling; and Emett, silent man of the desert, let from his wide cavernous chest a booming roar that drowned ours.

Jones' next decisive action turned us from exultation to the grim business of the thing. He pulled

Moze out of the cedar, and while he climbed up, Emett ran his rope under the collars of all of the hounds. Quick as the idea flashed over me I leaped into the cedar adjoining the one Jones was in, and went up hand over hand. A few pulls brought me to the top, and then my blood ran hot and quick, for I was level with the lion, too close for comfort, but in excellent position for taking pictures.

The lion, not heeding me, peered down at Jones, between widespread paws. I could hear nothing except the hounds. Jones' gray hat came pushing up between the dead snags; then his burly shoulders. The quivering muscles of the lion gathered tense, and his lithe body crouched low on the branches. He was about to jump. His open dripping jaws, his wild eyes, roving in terror for some means of escape, his tufted tail, swinging against the twigs and breaking them, manifested his extremity. The eager hounds waited below, howling, leaping.

It bothered me considerably to keep my balance, regulate my camera and watch the proceedings. Jones climbed on with his rope between his teeth, and a long stick. The very next instant it seemed to me, I heard the cracking of branches and saw the lion biting hard at the noose which circled his neck.

Here I swung down, branch to branch, and dropped to the ground, for I wanted to see what went on below. Above the howls and yelps, I distinguished Jones' yell. Emett ran directly under the lion with a spread noose in his hands. Jones pulled and pulled, but the lion held on firmly. Throwing the end of the lasso down to Jim, Jones yelled again, and then they both pulled. The lion was too strong. Suddenly, however, the branch broke, letting the lion fall, kicking frantically with all four paws. Emett grasped one of the four whipping paws, and even as the powerful animal sent him staggering he dexterously left the noose fast on the paw. Jim and Jones in unison let go of their lasso, which streaked up through the branches as the lion fell, and then it dropped to the ground, where Jim made a flying grab for it. Jones plunging out of the tree fell upon the rope at the same instant.

If the action up to then had been fast, it was slow to what followed. It seemed impossible for two strong men with one lasso, and a giant with another, to straighten out that lion. He was all over the little space under the trees at once. The dust flew, the sticks snapped, the gravel pattered like shot against the cedars. Jones ploughed the ground flat on his stomach, holding on with one hand, with the other trying to fasten the rope to something; Jim went to his knees; and on the other side of the lion, Emett's huge bulk tipped a sharp angle, and then fell.

I shouted and ran forward, having no idea what to do, but Emett rolled backward, at the same instant the other men got a strong haul on the lion. Short as that moment was in which the lasso slackened, it sufficed for Jones to make the rope fast to a tree. Whereupon with the three men pulling on the other side of the leaping lion, somehow I had flashed into my mind the game that children play, called skipping the rope, for the lion and lasso shot up and down.

This lasted for only a few seconds. They stretched the beast from tree to tree, and Jones running with the third lasso, made fast the front paws.

"It's a female," said Jones, as the lion lay helpless, her sides swelling; "a good-sized female. She's nearly eight feet from tip to tip, but not very heavy. Hand me another rope."

When all four lassos had been stretched, the lioness could not move. Jones strapped a collar around her neck and clipped the sharp yellow claws.

"Now to muzzle her," he continued.

Jones' method of performing this most hazardous part of the work was characteristic of him. He thrust a stick between her open jaws, and when she crushed it to splinters he tried another, and yet another, until he found one that she could not break. Then while she bit on it, he placed a wire loop over her nose, slowly tightening it, leaving the stick back of her big canines.

The hounds ceased their yelping and when untied, Sounder wagged his tail as if to say, "Well done," and then lay down; Don walked within three feet of the lion, as if she were now beneath his dignity; Jude began to nurse and lick her sore paw; only Moze the incorrigible retained antipathy for the captive, and he growled, as always, low and deep. And on the moment, Ranger, dusty and lame from travel, trotted wearily into the glade and, looking at the lioness, gave one disgusted bark and flopped down.

III

Transporting our captives to camp bade fair to make us work. When Jones, who had gone after the pack horses, hove in sight on the sage flat, it was plain to us that we were in for trouble. The bay stallion was on the rampage.

"Why didn't you fetch the Indian?" growled Emett,

who lost his temper when matters concerning his horses went wrong. "Spread out, boys, and head him off."

We contrived to surround the stallion, and Emett succeeded in getting a halter on him.

"I didn't want the bay," explained Jones, "but I couldn't drive the others without him. When I told that redskin that we had two lions, he ran off into the woods, so I had to come alone."

"I'm going to scalp the Navajo," said Jim, complacently.

These remarks were exchanged on the open ridge at the entrance to the thick cedar forest. The two lions lay just within its shady precincts. Emett and I, using a long pole in lieu of a horse, had carried Tom up from the Canyon to where we had captured the lioness.

Jones had brought a packsaddle and two panniers. When Emett essayed to lead the horse which carried these, the animal stood straight up and began to show some of his primal desert instincts. It certainly was good luck that we unbuckled the packsaddle straps before he left the vicinity. In about three jumps he had separated himself from the panniers, which were then placed upon the back of another horse. This one, a fine looking beast, and amiable under surroundings where his life and health were considered even a little, immediately disclaimed any intention of entering the forest.

"They scent the lions," said Jones. "I was afraid of it; never had but one nag that would pack lions."

"Maybe we can't pack them at all," replied Emett dubiously. "It's certainly new to me."

"We've got to," Jones asserted; "try the sorrel."

For the first time in a serviceable and honorable life, according to Emett, the sorrel broke his halter and kicked like a plantation mule.

"It's a matter of fright. Try the stallion. He doesn't look afraid," said Jones, who never knew when he was beaten.

Emett gazed at Jones as if he had not heard right.

"Go ahead, try the stallion. I like the way he looks."

No wonder! The big stallion looked a king of horses—just what he would have been if Emett had not taken him, when a colt, from his wild desert brothers. He scented the lions, and he held his proud head up, his ears erect, and his large, dark eyes shone fiery and expressive.

"I'll try to lead him in and let him see the lions. We can't fool him," said Emett.

Marc showed no hesitation, nor anything we expected. He stood stiff-legged, and looked as if he wanted to fight.

"He's all right; he'll pack them," declared Jones.

The packsaddle being strapped on and the panniers hooked to the horns, Jones and Jim lifted Tom and shoved him down into the left pannier while Emett held the horse. A madder lion than Tom never lived. It was cruel enough to be lassoed and disgrace enough to be "hog-tied," as Jim called it, but to be thrust down into a bag and packed on a horse was adding insult to injury. Tom frothed at the mouth and seemed like a fizzing torpedo about to explode. The lioness being considerably longer and larger, was with difficulty gotten into the other pannier, and her head and paws hung out. Both lions kept growling and snarling.

"I look to see Marc bolt over the rim," said Emett, resignedly, as Jones took up the end of the rope halter.

"No siree!" sang out that worthy. "He's helping us out; he's proud to show up the other nags."

Jones was always asserting strange traits in animals, and giving them intelligence and reason. As to that, many incidents coming under my observation while with him, and seen with his eyes, made me incline to his claims, the fruit of a lifetime with animals.

Marc packed the lions to camp in short order, and, quoting Jones, "without turning a hair." We saw the Navajo's head protruding from a tree. Emett yelled for him, and Jones and Jim "hahaed" derisively; whereupon the black head vanished and did not reappear. Then they unhooked one of the panniers and dumped out the lioness. Jones fastened her chain to a small pine tree, and as she lay powerless he pulled out the stick back of her canines. This allowed the wire muzzle to fall off. She signalled this freedom with a roar that showed her health to be still unimpaired. The last action in releasing her from her painful bonds Jones performed with sleight-of-hand dexterity. He slipped the loop fastening one paw, which loosened the rope, and in a twinkling let her work all of her other paws free. Up she sprang, ears flat, eyes ablaze, mouth wide, once more capable of defense, true to her instinct and her name.

Before the men lowered Tom from Marc's back I stepped closer and put my face within six inches of the lion's. He promptly spat on me. I had to steel my nerve to keep so close. But I wanted to see a wild lion's eyes at close range. They were exquisitely beautiful, their physical properties as wonderful as their expression. Great half globes of tawny amber, streaked with delicate wavy lines of black, surrounding pupils of intense purple fire. Pictures shone and faded in the amber light—the shaggy tipped plateau, the dark pines and smoky canyons, the great dotted downward slopes, the yellow cliffs and crags. Deep in those live pupils, changing, quickening with a thousand vibrations, quivered the soul of this savage beast, the wildest of all wild Nature, unquenchable love of life and freedom, flame of defiance and hate.

Jones disposed of Tom in the same manner as he had the lioness, chaining him to an adjoining small pine, where he leaped and wrestled.

Presently I saw Emett coming through the woods leading and dragging the Indian. I felt sorry for the Navvy, for I felt that his fear was not so much physical as spiritual. And it seemed no wonder to me that the Navvy should hang back from this sacrilegious treatment of his god. A natural wisdom, which I had in common with all human beings who consider self preservation the first law of life, deterred me from acquainting my august companions with my belief. At least I did not want to break up the camp.

In the remorseless grasp of Emett, forced along, the Navajo dragged his feet and held his face sidewise, though his dark eyes gleamed at the lions. Terror predominated among the expressions of his countenance. Emett drew him within fifteen feet and held him there, and with voice, and gesticulating of his free hand, tried to show the poor fellow that the lions would not hurt him.

Navvy stared and muttered to himself. Here Jim had some deviltry in mind, for he edged up closer;

but what it was never transpired, for Emett suddenly pointed to the horses and said to the Indian:

"*Chineago* (feed)."

It appeared when Navvy swung himself over Marc's broad back, that our great stallion had laid aside his transiently noble disposition and was himself again. Marc proceeded to show us how truly Jim had spoken: "Shore he ain't no use for the redskin." Before the Indian had fairly gotten astride, Marc dropped his head, humped his shoulders, brought his feet together and began to buck. Now the Navajo was a famous breaker of wild mustangs, but Marc was a tougher proposition than the wildest mustang that ever romped the desert. Not only was he unusually vigorous; he was robust and heavy, yet exceedingly active. I had seen him roll over in the dust three times each way, and do it easily—a feat Emett declared he had never seen performed by another horse.

Navvy began to bounce. He showed his teeth and twisted his sinewy hands in the horse's mane. Marc began to act like a demon; he plowed the ground; apparently he bucked five feet straight up. As the Indian had bounced he now began to shoot into the air. He rose the last time with his heels over his head, to the full extent of his arms; and on plunging down his hold broke. He spun around the horse, then went hurtling to the ground some twenty feet away. He sat up, and seeing Emett and Jones laughing, and Jim prostrated with joy, he showed his white teeth in a smile and said:

"No bueno dam."

I think all of us respected Navvy for his good humor, and especially when he walked up to Marc, and with no show of the mean Indian, patted the glossy neck and then nimbly remounted. Marc, not being so difficult to please as Jim in the way of discomfiting the Navajo, appeared satisfied for the present, and trotted off down the hollow, with the string of horses ahead, their bells jingling.

Camp-fire tasks were a necessary wage in order to earn the full enjoyment and benefit of the hunting trip; and looking for some task with which to turn my hand, I helped Jim feed the hounds. To feed ordinary dogs is a matter of throwing them a bone; however, our dogs were not ordinary. It took time to feed them, and a prodigious amount of meat. We had packed between three and four hundred pounds of wild-horse meat, which had been cut into small pieces and strung on the branches of a scrub oak near camp.

Don, as befitted a gentleman and the leader of the greatest pack in the West, had to be fed by hand. I believe he would rather had starved than have demeaned himself by fighting. Starved he certainly would have, if Jim had thrown meat indiscriminately to the ground. Sounder asserted his rights and preferred large portions at a time. Jude begged with great solemn eyes but was no slouch at eating for all her gentleness. Ranger, because of imperfectly developed teeth rendering mastication difficult, had to have his share cut into very small pieces. As for Moze—well, great dogs have their faults as do great men—he never got enough meat; he would fight even poor crippled Jude, and steal even from the pups; when he had gotten all Jim would give him, and all he could snatch, he would growl away with bulging sides.

"How about feeding the lions?" asked Emett.

"They'll drink to-night," replied Jones, "but won't eat for days; then we'll tempt them with fresh rabbits."

We made a hearty meal, succeeding which Jones and I walked through the woods toward the rim. A yellow promontory, huge and glistening, invited us westward, and after a detour of half a mile we reached it. The points of the rim, striking out into the immense void, always drew me irresistibly. We found the view from this rock one of startling splendor. The corrugated rim-wall of the middle wing extended to the west, at this moment apparently running into the setting sun. The gold glare touching up the millions of facets of chiseled stone, created color and brilliance too glorious and intense for the gaze of men. And looking downward was like looking into the placid, blue, bottomless depths of the Pacific.

"Here, help me push off this stone," I said to Jones. We heaved a huge round stone, and were encouraged to feel it move. Fortunately we had a little slope; the boulder groaned, rocked and began to slide. Just as it toppled over I glanced at the second hand of my watch. Then with eyes over the rim we waited. The silence was the silence of the canyon, dead and vast, intensified by our breathless earstrain. Ten long palpitating seconds and no sound! I gave up. The distance was too great for sound to reach us. Fifteen seconds—seventeen—eighteen—

With that a puff of air seemed to rise, and on it the most awful bellow of thunderous roar. It rolled up and widened, deadened to burst out and roll louder, then slowly, like mountains on wheels, rumbled under the rim-walls, passing on and on, to roar back in echo from the cliffs of the mesas. Roar and rumble—roar and rumble! for two long moments the dull and hollow echoes rolled at us, to die away slowly in the far-distant canyons.

"That's a darned deep hole," commented Jones.

Twilight stole down on us idling there, silent, content to watch the red glow pass away from the buttes and peaks, the color deepening downward to meet the ebon shades of night creeping up like a dark tide.

On turning toward the camp we essayed a short cut, which brought us to a deep hollow with stony walls, which seemed better to go around. The hollow, however, was quite long and we decided presently to cross it. We descended a little way when Jones suddenly barred my progress with his big arm.

"Listen," he whispered.

It was quiet in the woods; only a faint breeze stirred the pine needles; and the weird, gray darkness seemed to be approaching under the trees.

I heard the patter of light, hard hoofs on the scaly sides of the hollow.

"Deer?" I asked my companion in a low voice.

"Yes; see," he replied, pointing ahead, "just right under that broken wall of rock; right there on this side; they're going down."

I descried gray objects the color of the rocks, moving down like shadows.

"Have they scented us?"

"Hardly; the breeze is against us. Maybe they heard us break a twig. They've stopped, but they are not looking our way. Now I wonder—"

Rattling of stones set into movement by some quick, sharp action, an indistinct crash, but sudden, as of the impact of soft, heavy bodies, a strange wild sound preceded in rapid succession violent brushings and thumpings in the scrub of the hollow.

"Lion jumped a deer," yelled Jones. "Right under our eyes! Come on! Hi! Hi! Hi!"

He ran down the incline yelling all of the way, and I kept close to him, adding my yells to his, and gripping my revolver. Toward the bottom the thicket barred our progress so that we had to smash through and I came out a little ahead of Jones. And farther up the hollow I saw a gray swiftly bounding object too long and too low for a deer, and I hurriedly shot six times at it.

"By George! Come here," called my companion. "How's this for quick work? It's a yearling doe."

In another moment I leaned over a gray mass huddled at Jones feet. It was a deer gasping and choking. I plainly heard the wheeze of blood in its throat, and the sound, like a death-rattle, affected me powerfully. Bending closer, I saw where one side of the neck, low down, had been terribly lacerated.

"Waa-hoo!" pealed down the slope.

"That's Emett," cried Jones, answering the signal. "If you have another shot put this doe out of agony."

But I had not a shot left, nor did either of us have a clasp knife. We stood there while the doe gasped and quivered. The peculiar sound, probably made by the intake of air through the laceration of the throat, on the spur of the moment seemed pitifully human.

I felt that the struggle for life and death in any living thing was a horrible spectacle. With great interest I had studied natural selection, the variability of animals under different conditions of struggling existence, the law whereby one animal struck down and devoured another. But I had never seen and heard that law enacted on such a scale; and suddenly I abhorred it.

Emett strode to us through the gathering darkness.

"What's up?" he asked quickly.

He carried my Remington in one hand and his Winchester in the other; and he moved so assuredly and loomed up so big in the dusk that I experienced a sudden little rush of feeling as to what his advent might mean at a time of real peril.

"Emett, I've lived to see many things," replied Jones, "but this is the first time I ever saw a lion jump a deer right under my nose!"

As Emett bent over to seize the long ears of the deer, I noticed the gasping had ceased.

"Neck broken," he said, lifting the head. "Well, I'm danged. Must have been an all-fired strong lion. He'll come back, you may be sure of that. Let's skin out the quarters and hang the carcass up in a tree!"

We returned to camp in a half an hour, the richer for our walk by a quantity of fresh venison. Upon being acquainted with our adventure, Jim expressed himself rather more fairly than was his customary way.

"Shore that beats hell! I knowed there was a lion somewheres, because Don wouldn't lie down. I'd like to get a pop at the brute."

I believed Jim's wish found an echo in all our hearts. At any rate to hear Emett and Jones express regret over the death of the doe justified in some degree my own feelings, and I thought it was not so much the death, but the lingering and terrible manner of it, and especially how vividly it connoted the wild-life drama of the plateau. The tragedy we had all but interrupted occurred every night, perhaps often in the day and likely at different points at the same time. Emett told how he had found fourteen piles of bleached bones and dried hair in the thickets of less than a mile of the hollow on which we were encamped.

"We'll rope the danged cats, boys, or we'll kill them."

"It's blowing cold. Hey, Navvy, *coco! coco!*" called Emett.

The Indian, carefully laying aside his cigarette, kicked up the fire and threw on more wood.

"*Discass!* (cold)," he said to me. "*Coco, bueno* (fire good)."

I replied, "Me savvy—yes."

"Sleep-ie?" he asked.

"Mucha," I returned.

While we carried on a sort of novel conversation full of Navajo, English, and gestures, darkness settled down black. I saw the stars disappear; the wind changing to the north grew colder and carried a breath of snow. I like north wind best—from under the warm blankets—because of the roar and lull and lull and roar in the pines. Crawling into the bed presently, I lay there and listened to the rising stormwind for a long time. Sometimes it swelled and crashed like the sound of a breaker on the beach, but mostly, from a low incessant moan, it rose and filled to a mighty rush, then suddenly lulled. This lull, despite a wakeful, thronging mind, was conducive to sleep.

Grey and Nasja Begay, the Piute Indian guide who led the first white men, Cummings and Wetherill, to Rainbow Bridge in 1909, and then Grey in 1913.

One of the Southwest's most awesome sights—a ten-foot wall of water rushing through a dry wash during a flash flood.

Pack train going through the Glass Mountains on the way to Rainbow Bridge. It was necessary to lead horses through this entire stretch because of sudden sharp gusts of wind that could blow horse and rider over the steep cliffs.

Grey at Nonnezoshe.

Zane Grey looking at the huge natural cave that contains the ruins of Betatakin, an ancient Indian village first discovered by the Cummings/ Wetherill expedition in 1909.

Grey is dwarfed by the looming arch of Nonnezoshe (Rainbow Bridge).

Zane Grey after two months in the wild.

Looking down on cloud-filled valleys.

In a meadow below Flattop Mountain, Colorado.

Searching burned-over ranges for game.

A black bear treed.

Zane Grey and his brother, R.C., on the Colorado River at the bottom of the Grand Canyon.

Jim Emett, pioneer guide for Zane Grey and Buffalo Jones in the first mountain lion hunting expedition. Emett became the prototype for August Naab, great Mormon leader in Heritage of the Desert.

Navvy, Indian guide on Jones' expedition.

Mountain lion hiding on a rock ledge.

Treed lion.

Buffalo Jones climbing the tree to lasso the lion.

Zane Grey holding one of the ropes that restrained the captured lion.

A chained lion paws the tree trunk.

Buffalo Jones with one of the captured lions.

Captured lions in camp.

Jones, Emett, and Navvy loading a lion on a pack horse.

Looking upslope for game.

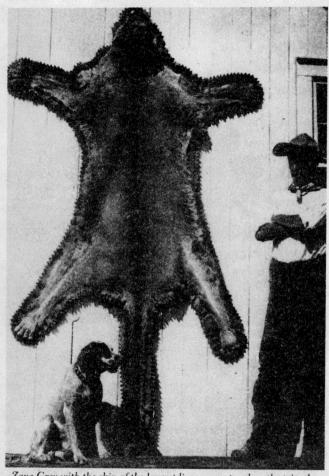
Zane Grey with the skin of the largest lion encountered on the trip; the lion hung himself over a tree branch after being lassoed.

IV

To be awaked from pleasant dreams is the lot of man. The Navajo aroused me with his singing, and when I peeped languidly from under the flap of my sleeping bag, I felt a cold air and saw fleecy flakes of white drifting through the small window of my tent.

"Snow; by all that's lucky!" I exclaimed, remembering Jones' hopes. Straightway my langour vanished and getting into my boots and coat I went outside. Navvy's bed lay in six inches of snow. The forest was beautifully white. A fine dazzling snow was falling. I walked to the roaring camp-fire. Jim's biscuits, well-browned and of generous size, had just been dumped into the middle of our breakfast cloth, a tarpaulin spread on the ground; the coffee pot steamed fragrantly, and a Dutch oven sizzled with a great number of slices of venison.

"Did you hear the Indian chanting?" asked Jones, who sat with his horny hands to the blaze.

"I heard his singing."

"No, it wasn't a song; the Navajo never sings in the morning. What you heard was his morning prayer, a chant, a religious and solemn ritual to the break of day. Emett says it is a custom of the desert tribe. You remember how we saw the Mokis sitting on the roofs of their little adobe huts in the gray of the morning. They always greet the sun in that way. The Navajos chant."

It certainly was worth remembering, I thought, and mentally observed that I would wake up thereafter and listen to the Indian.

"Good luck and bad!" went on Jones. "Snow is

what we want, but now we can't find the scent of
our lion of last night."

Low growls and snarls attracted me. Both our
captives presented sorry spectacles; they were wet,
dirty, bedraggled. Emett had chopped down a small
pine, the branches of which he was using to make
shelter for the lions. While I looked on Tom tore his
to pieces several times, but the lioness crawled under
hers and began licking her chops. At length Tom,
seeing that Emett meant no underhand trick, backed
out of the drizzling snow and lay down.

Emett had already constructed a shack for the
hounds. It was a way of his to think of everything.
He had the most extraordinary ability. A stroke of
his axe, a twist of his great hands, a turn of this or
that made camp a more comfortable place. And if
something, no matter what, got out of order or broken, there was Emett to show what it was to be a
man of the desert. It had been my good fortune to
see many able men on the trail and round the camp-
fire, but not one of them even approached Emett's
class. When I said a word to him about his knack
with things, his reply was illuminating: "I'm fifty-
eight, and four out of every five nights of my life I
have slept away from home on the ground."

"*Chineago!*" called Jim, who had begun with all
of us to assimilate a little of the Navajo's language.

Whereupon we fell to eating with appetite unknown to any save hunters. Somehow the Indian had
gravitated to me at meal times, and now he sat
cross-legged beside me, holding out his plate and
looking as hungry as Moze. At first he had always
asked for the same kind of food that I happened to
have on my own plate. When I had finished and had

no desire to eat more, he gave up his faculty of imitation and asked for anything he could get. The Navajo had a marvelous appetite. He liked sweet things, sugar best of all. It was a fatal error to let him get his hands on a can of fruit. Although he inspired Jones with disgust and Jim with worse, he was a source of unfailing pleasure to me. He called me "Mista Gay" and he pronounced the words haltingly in low voice and with unmistakable respect.

"What's on for today?" queried Emett.

"I guess we may as well hang around camp and rest the hounds," replied Jones. "I did intend to go after the lion that killed the deer, but this snow has taken away the scent."

"Shore it'll stop snowin' soon," said Jim.

The falling snow had thinned out and looked like flying powder; the leaden clouds, rolling close to the treetops, grew brighter and brighter; bits of azure sky shone through rifts.

Navvy had tramped off to find the horses, and not long after his departure he sent out a prolonged yell that echoed through the forest.

"Something's up," said Emett instantly. "An Indian never yells like that at a horse."

We waited quietly for a moment, expecting to hear the yell repeated. It was not, though we soon heard the jangle of bells, which told us he had the horses coming. He appeared off to the right, riding Foxie and racing the others toward camp.

"Cougie—mucha big—dam!" he said leaping off the mustang to confront us.

"Emett, does he mean he saw a cougar or a track?" questioned Jones.

"Me savvy," replied the Indian. *"Butteen, but-teen!"*

"He says, trail—trail," put in Emett. "I guess I'd better go and see."

"I'll go with you," said Jones. "Jim, keep the hounds tight and hurry with the horses' oats."

We followed the tracks of the horses which lead southwest toward the rim, and a quarter of a mile from camp we crossed a lion trail running at right angles with our direction.

"Old Sultan!" I cried, breathlessly, recognizing that the tracks had been made by a giant lion we had named Sultan. They were huge, round, and deep, and with my spread hand I could not reach across one of them.

Without a word, Jones strode off on the trail. It headed east and after a short distance turned toward camp. I suppose Jones knew what the lion had been about, but to Emett and me it was mystifying. Two hundred yards from camp we came to a fallen pine, the body of which was easily six feet high. On the side of this log, almost on top, were two enormous lion tracks, imprinted in the mantle of snow. From here the trail led off northeast.

"Darn me!" ejaculated Jones. "The big critter came right into camp; he scented our lions, and raised up on this log to look over."

Wheeling, he started for camp on the trot. Emett and I kept even with him. Words were superfluous. We knew what was coming. A made-to-order lion trail could not have equalled the one right in the back yard of our camp.

"Saddle up!" said Jones, with the sharp inflection

of words that had come to thrill me. "Jim, Old Sultan has taken a look at us since break of day."

I got into my chaps, rammed my little automatic into its saddle holster and mounted. Foxie seemed to want to go. The hounds came out of their sheds and yawned, looking at us knowingly. Emett spoke a word to the Navajo, and then we were trotting down through the forest. The sun had broken out warm, causing water to drip off the snow laden pines. The three of us rode close behind Jones, who spoke low and sternly to the hounds.

What an opportunity to watch Don! I wondered how soon he would catch the scent of the trail. He led the pack as usual and kept to a leisurely dog-trot. When within twenty yards of the fallen log, he stopped for an instant and held up his head, though without exhibiting any suspicion or uneasiness.

The wind blew strong at our backs, a circumstance that probably kept Don so long in ignorance of the trail. A few yards further on, however, he stopped and raised his fine head. He lowered it and trotted on only to stop again. His easy air of satisfaction with the morning suddenly vanished. His savage hunting instinct awakened through some channel to raise the short yellow hair on his neck and shoulders and make it stand stiff. He stood undecided with warily shifting nose, then jumped forward with a yelp. Another jump brought another sharp cry from him. Sounder, close behind, echoed the yelp. Jude began to whine. Then Don, with a wild howl, leaped ten feet to alight on the lion trail and to break into wonderfully rapid flight. The seven other hounds, bunched in a black and yellow group, tore after him filling the forest with their wild uproar.

Emett's horse bounded as I have seen a great racer leave the post, and his desert brothers, loving wild bursts of speed, needing no spur, kept their noses even with his flanks. The soft snow, not too deep, rather facilitated than impeded this wild movement, and the open forest was like a highway.

So we rode, bending low in the saddle, keen eyes alert for branches, vaulting the white-blanketed logs, and swerving as we split to pass the pines. The mist from the melting snow moistened our faces, and the rushing air cooled them with fresh, soft sensation. There were moments when we rode abreast and others when we sailed single file, with white ground receding, vanishing behind us.

My feeling was one of glorious excitation in the swift, smooth flight and a grim assurance of soon seeing the old lion. But I hoped we would not rout him too soon from under a windfall, or a thicket where he had dragged a deer, because the race was too splendid a thing to cut short. Through my mind whirled with inconceivable rapidity the great lion chases on which we had ridden the year before. And this was another chase, only more stirring, more beautiful, because it was the nature of the thing to grow always with experience.

Don slipped out of sight among the pines. The others strung along the trail, glinted across the sunlit patches. The black pup was neck and neck with Ranger. Sounder ran at their heels, leading the other pups. Moze dashed on doggedly ahead of Jude.

But for us to keep to the open forest, close to the hounds, was not in the nature of a lion chase. Old Sultan's trail turned due west when he began to go down the little hollows and their intervening ridges.

We lost ground. The pack left us behind. The slope of the plateau became decided. We rode out of the pines to find the snow failing in the open. Water ran in little gullies and glistened on the sagebrush. A half mile further down the snow had gone. We came upon the hounds running at fault, except Sounder, and he had given up.

"All over," sang out Jones, turning his horse. "The lion's track and his scent have gone with the snow. I reckon we'll do as well to wait until tomorrow. He's down in the middle wing somewhere and it is my idea we might catch his trail as he comes back."

The sudden dashing aside of our hopes was exasperating. There seemed no help for it; abrupt ending to exciting chases were but features of the lion hunt. The warm sun had been hours on the lower end of the plateau, where the snow never lay long; and even if we found a fresh morning trail in the sand, the heat would have burned out the scent.

So rapidly did the snow thaw that by the time we reached camp only the shady patches were left.

It was almost eleven o'clock when I lay down on my bed to rest awhile and fell asleep. The tramp of a horse awakened me. I heard Jim calling Jones. Thinking it was time to eat I went out. The snow had all disappeared and the forest was brown as ever. Jim sat on his horse and Navvy appeared riding up to the hollow, leading the saddle horses.

"Jones, get out," called Jim.

"Can't you let a fellow sleep? I'm not hungry," replied Jones testily.

"Get out and saddle up," continued Jim.

Jones burst out of his tent, with rumpled hair and sleepy eyes.

"I went over to see the carcass of the deer an' found a lion sittin' up in the tree, feedin' for all he was worth. He jumped out an' ran up the hollow an' over the rim. So I rustled back for you fellows. Lively now, we'll get this one sure."

"Was it the big fellow?" I asked.

"No, but he ain't no kitten; an' he's a fine color, sort of reddish. I never seen one just as bright. Where's Emett?"

"I don't know. He was here a little while ago. Shall I signal for him?"

"Don't yell," cried Jones holding up his fingers. "Be quiet now."

Without another word we finished saddling, mounted and, close together, with the hounds in front, rode through the forest toward the rim.

V

We rode in different directions toward the hollow, the better to chance meeting with Emett, but none of us caught a glimpse of him.

It happened that when we headed into the hollow it was at a point just above where the deer carcass hung in the scrub oak. Don in spite of Jones' stern yells, let out his eager hunting yelp and darted down the slope. The pack bolted after him and in less than ten seconds were racing up the hollow, their thrilling, blending bays a welcome spur to action. Though I spoke not a word to my mustang nor had time to raise the bridle, he wheeled to one side and began to run. The other horses also kept to the ridge, as I

could tell by the pounding of hoofs on the soft turf.
The hounds in full cry right under us urged our good
steeds to a terrific pace. It was well that the ridge
afforded clear going.

The speed at which we traveled, however, fast as
it was, availed not to keep up with the pack. In a
short half mile, just as the hollow sloped and merged
into level ground, they left us behind and disappeared so quickly as almost to frighten me. My
mustang plunged out of the forest to the rim and
dashed along, apparently unmindful of the chasm.
The red and yellow surface blurred in a blinding
glare. I heard the chorus of hounds, but as its direction baffled me I trusted to my horse and I did well,
for soon he came to a dead halt on the rim.

Then I heard the hounds below me. I had but time
to see the character of the place—long, yellow promontories running out and slopes of weathered stone
reaching up between to a level with the rim—when
in a dwarf pine growing just over the edge I caught
sight of a long, red, pantherish body.

I whooped to my followers now close upon me
and leaping off hauled out my Remington and ran to
the cliff. The lion's long, slender body, of a rare
golden-red color, bright, clean, black-tipped and white-
bellied, proclaimed it a female of exceeding beauty.
I could have touched her with a fishing rod and saw
how easily she could be roped from where I stood.
The tree in which she had taken refuge grew from
the head of a weathered slope and rose close to the
wall. At that point it was merely a parapet of crumbling yellow rock. No doubt she had lain concealed
under the shelving wall and had not had time to get
away before the hounds were right upon her.

"She's going to jump," yelled Jones, in my rear, as he dismounted.

I saw a golden-red streak flash downward, heard a mad medley from the hounds, a cloud of dust rose, then something bright shone for a second to the right along the wall. I ran with all my might to a headland of rock upon which I scrambled and saw with joy that I could command the situation.

The lioness was not in sight, nor were the hounds. The latter, however, were hot on the trail. I knew the lioness had taken to another tree or a hole under the wall, and would soon be routed out. This time I felt sure she would run down and I took a rapid glance below. The slope inclined at a steep angle and was one long slide of bits of yellow stone with many bunches of scrub oak and manzanita. Those latter I saw with satisfaction, because in case I had to go down they would stop the little avalanches. The slope reached down perhaps five hundred yards and ended in a thicket and jumble of rocks from which rose on the right a bare yellow slide. This ran up to a low cliff. I hoped the lion would not go that way, for it led to great broken battlements of rim. Left of the slide was a patch of cedars.

Jim's yell pealed out, followed by the familiar penetrating howl of the pack when it sighted game. With that I saw the lioness leaping down the slope and close behind her a yellow hound.

"Go it, Don, old boy!" I yelled, wild with delight.

A crushing step on the stones told me Jones had arrived.

"Hi! Hi! Hi!" roared he.

I thought then that if the lioness did not cover thirty feet at every jump I was not in a condition to judge distance. She ran away from Don as if he had been tied and reached the thicket below a hundred yards ahead of him. And when Don leaving his brave pack far up the slide entered the thicket the lioness came out on the other side and bounded up the bare slope of yellow shale.

"Shoot ahead of her! Head her off! Turn her back!" cried Jones.

With the word I threw forward the Remington and let drive. Following the bellow of the rifle, so loud in that thin air, a sharp, harsh report cracked up from below. A puff of yellow dust rose in front of the lioness. I was in line, but too far ahead. I fired again. The steel jacketed bullet hit a stone and spitefully whined away into the canyon. I tried once more. This time I struck close to the lioness. Disconcerted by a cloud of dust rising before her very eyes she wheeled and ran back.

We had forgotten Don and suddenly he darted out of the thicket, straight up the slide. Always, in every chase, we were afraid the great hound would run to meet his death. We knew it was coming sometime. When the lioness saw him and stopped, both Jones and I felt that this was to be the end of Don.

"Shoot her! Shoot her!" cried Jones. "She'll kill him! She'll kill him!"

As I knelt on the rock I had a hard contraction of my throat, and then all my muscles set tight and rigid. I pulled the trigger of my automatic once, twice. It was wonderful how closely the two bullets followed each other, as we could tell by the almost simultaneous puffs of dust rising from under the beast's nose. She must have been showered and stung with gravel, for she bounded off to the left and disappeared in the cedars. I had missed, but the shots had served to a better end than if I had killed her.

As Don raced up the ground where a moment before a battle and probably death had awaited him, the other hounds burst from the thicket. With that, a golden form seemed to stand out from the green of the cedar, to move and to rise.

"She's treed! She's treed!" shouted Jones. "Go down and keep her there while I follow."

From the back of the promontory where I met the main wall, I let myself down a niche, foot here and there, a hand hard on the soft stone, braced knee and back until I jumped to the edge of the slope. The scrub oak and manzanita saved me many a fall. I set some stones rolling and I beat them to the bottom. Having passed the thicket, I bent my efforts to the yellow slide and when I had surmounted it my breath came in labored pants. The howling of the hounds guided me through the cedars.

First I saw Moze in the branches of cedar and above him the lioness. I ran out into a little open patch of stony ground at the end of which the tree stood leaning over a precipice. In truth the lioness was swaying over a chasm.

Those details I grasped in a glance, then suddenly awoke to the fact that the lioness was savagely snarling at Moze.

"Moze! Moze! Get down!" I yelled.

He climbed on serenely. He was a most exasperating dog. I screamed at him and hit him with a rock big enough to break his bones. He kept on climbing. Here was a predicament. Moze would surely get to the lioness if I did not stop him, and this seemed impossible. It was out of the question for me to climb after him. And if the lioness jumped she would have to pass me or come straight at me. So I slipped down the safety catch on my automatic and stood ready to save Moze or myself.

The lioness with a show of fury that startled me, descended her branch a few steps, and reaching below gave Moze a sounding smack with her big paw. The hound dropped as if he had been shot and hit the ground with a thud. Whereupon she returned to her perch.

This reassured me and I ran among the dogs and caught Moze already starting for the tree again and tied him, with a strap I always carried, to a small bush nearby. I heard the yells of my companions and looking back over the tops of the cedars I saw Jim riding down and higher to the left Jones sliding, falling, running at a great rate. I encouraged them to keep up the good work, and then gave my attention to the lioness.

She regarded me with a cold, savage stare and showed her teeth. I repaid this incivility on her part by promptly photographing her from different points.

Jones and Jim were on the spot before I expected them and both were dusty and dripping with sweat. I found to my surprise that my face was wet as was also my shirt. Jones carried two lassos, and my canteen, which I had left on the promontory.

"Ain't she a beauty?" he panted, wiping his face. "Wait—till I get my breath."

When finally he walked toward the cedar the lioness stood up and growled as if she realized the entrance of the chief actor upon the scene. Jones cast his lasso apparently to try her out, and the noose spread out and fell over her head. As he tightened the rope the lioness backed down behind a branch.

"Tie the dogs!" yelled Jones.

"Quick!" added Jim. "She's goin to jump."

Jim had only time to aid me in running my lasso under the collar of Don, Sounder, Jude and one of the pups. I made them fast to a cedar. I got my hands on Ranger just as Moze broke his strap. I grabbed his collar and held on.

Right there was where trouble commenced for me. Ranger tussled valiantly and Moze pulled me all over the place. Behind me I heard Jones' roar and Jim's yell; the breaking of branches, the howling of the other dogs. Ranger broke away from me and so enabled me to get my other hand on the neck of crazy Moze. On more than one occasion I had tried to hold him and had failed; this time I swore I would do it if he rolled me over the precipice. As to that, only a bush saved me.

More and louder roars and yells, hoarser howls and sharper wrestling, snapping sounds told me what was going on while I tried to subdue Moze. I had a grim thought that I would just as lief have had hold of the lioness. The hound presently stopped his plunging which gave me an opportunity to look about. The little space was smoky with a smoke of dust. I saw the lioness stretched out with one lasso around a bush and another around a cedar with the end in the hands of Jim. He looked as if he had dug up the ground. While he tied this lasso securely Jones proceeded to rope the dangerous front paws.

The hounds quieted down and I took advantage of this absence of tumult to get rid of Moze.

"Pretty lively," said Jones, spitting gravel as I

walked up. Sand and dust lay thick in his beard and blackened his face. "I tell you she made us root."

Either the lioness had been much weakened or choked, or Jones had unusual luck, for we muzzled her and tied up her paws in short order.

"Where's Ranger?" I asked suddenly, missing him from the panting hounds.

"I grabbed him by the heels when he tackled the lion, and I gave him a sling somewheres," replied Jim.

Ranger put in an appearance then under the cedars limping painfully.

"Jim, darn me, if I don't believe you pitched him over the precipice!" said Jones.

Examination proved this surmise to be correct. We saw where Ranger had slipped over a twenty-foot wall. If he had gone over just under the cedar where the depth was much greater he would never have come back.

"The hounds are choking with dust and heat," I said. When I poured just a little water from my canteen into the crown of my hat, the hounds began fighting around and over me and spilled the water.

"Behave, you coyotes!" I yelled. Either they were insulted or fully realized the exigency of the situation, for each one came up and gratefully lapped every drop of his portion.

"Shore, now comes the hell of it," said Jim appearing with a long pole. "Packin' the critter out."

An argument arose in regard to the best way up the slope, and by virtue of a majority we decided to try the direction Jim and I thought best. My companions led the way, carrying the lioness suspended on the pole. I brought up the rear, packing my rifle, camera, lasso, canteen and a chain.

It was killing work. We had to rest every few steps. Often we would fall. Jim laughed, Jones swore, and I groaned. Sometimes I had to drop my things to help my companions. So we toiled wearily up the loose, steep way.

"What's she shakin' like that for?" asked Jim suddenly.

Jones let down his end of the pole and turned quickly. Little tremors quivered over the lissome body of the lioness.

"She's dying," cried Jim, jerking out the stick between her teeth and slipping off the wire muzzle.

Her mouth opened and her frothy tongue lolled out. Jones pointed to her quivering sides and then raised her eyelids. We saw the eyes already glazing, solemnly fixed.

"She's gone," he said.

Very soon she lay inert and lifeless. Then we sat beside her without a word, and we could hardly for the moment have been more stunned and heartbroken if it had been the tragic death of one of our kind. In that wild environment, obsessed by the desire to capture those beautiful cats alive, the fateful ending of the successful chase was felt out of all proportion.

"Shore she's dead," said Jim. "And wasn't she a beauty? What was wrong?"

"The heat and lack of water," replied Jones. "She choked. What idiots we were! Why didn't we think to give her a drink."

So we passionately protested against our want of forethought, and looked again and again with the hope that she might come to. But death had stilled

the wild heart. We gave up presently, still did not
move on. We were exhausted, and all the while the
hounds lay panting on the rocks, the bees hummed,
the flies buzzed. The red colors of the upper walls
and the purple shades of the lower darkened silently.

VI

"Shore we can't set here all night," said Jim.
"Let's skin the lion an' feed the hounds."

The most astonishing thing in our eventful day
was the amount of meat stowed away by the dogs.
Lion flesh appealed to their appetites. If hungry
Moze had an ounce of meat, he had ten pounds. It
seemed a good opportunity to see how much the old
gladiator could eat; and Jim and I cut chunks of meat
as fast as possible. Moze gulped them with absolute
unconcern of such a thing as mastication. At length
he reached his limit, possibly for the first time in his
life, and looking longingly at a juicy red strip Jim
held out, he refused it with manifest shame. Then he
wobbled and fell down.

We called to him as we started to climb the slope,
but he did not come. Then the business of conquer-
ing that ascent of sliding stone absorbed all our
faculties and strength. Little headway could we have
made had it not been for the brush. We toiled up a
few feet only to slide back and so it went on until we
were weary of life.

When one by one we at last gained the rim and sat
there to recover breath, the sun was a half globe of
fire burning over the western ramparts. A red sunset
bathed the canyon in crimson, painting the walls,
tinting the shadows to resemble dropping mists of

blood. It was beautiful and enthralling to my eyes, but I turned away because it wore the mantle of tragedy.

Dispirited and worn out, we trooped into camp to find Emett and a steaming supper. Between bites the three of us related the story of the red lioness. Emett whistled long and low and then expressed his regret in no light terms.

"Roping wild steers and mustangs is play to this work," he said in conclusion.

I was too tired to tease our captive lions that evening; even the glowing camp-fire tempted me in vain, and I crawled into my bed with eyes already glued shut.

A heavy weight on my feet stirred me from oblivion. At first, when only half awake, I could not realize what had fallen on my bed, then hearing a deep groan I knew Moze had come back. I was dropping off again when a strange, low sound caused my eyes to open wide. The black night had faded to the gray of dawn. The sound I recognized at once to be the Navajo's morning chant. I lay there and listened. Soft and monotonous, wild and swelling, but always low and strange, the savage song to the break of day was exquisitely beautiful and harmonious. I wondered what the literal meaning of his words could have been. The significance needed no translation. To the black shadows fading away, to the brightening of the gray light, to the glow of the east, to the morning sun, to the Giver of Life—to these the Indian chanted his prayer.

Could there have been a better prayer? Pagan or not, the Navajo with his forefathers felt the spiritual power of the trees, the rocks, the light and sun, and he prayed to that which was divinely helpful to him in all the mystery of his unintelligible life.

We did not crawl out that morning as early as usual, for it was to be a day of rest. When we did, a mooted question arose—whether we or the hounds were the more crippled. Ranger did not show himself; Don could just walk and that was all; Moze was either too full or too tired to move; Sounder nursed a foot and Jude favored her lame leg.

After lunch we brightened up somewhat and set ourselves different tasks. Jones had misplaced or lost his wire and began to turn the camp topsy-turvy in his impatient efforts to locate it. The wire, however, was not to be found. This was a calamity, for, as we asked each other, how could we muzzle lions without wire? Moreover, a half dozen heavy leather straps which I had bought in Kanab for use as lion collars had disappeared. We had only one collar left, the one that Jones had put on the red lioness.

Whereupon we began to blame each other, to argue, to grow heated and naturally from that to become angry. It seems a fatality of campers along a wild trail, like explorers in an unknown land, to be prone to fight. If there is an explanation of this singular fact, it must be that men at such time lose their poise and veneer of civilization; in brief, they go back. At all events we had it hot and heavy, with the center of attack gradually focusing on Jones, and as he was always losing something, naturally we united in force against him.

Fortunately, we were interrupted by yells from the Navajo off in the woods. The brushing of branches and pounding of hoofs preceded his appearance. In some remarkable manner he had gotten a bridle on

Marc, and from the way the big stallion hurled his huge bulk over logs and through thickets, it appeared evident he meant to usurp Jim's ambition and kill the Navajo. Hearing Emett yell, the Indian turned Marc toward camp. The horse slowed down when he neared the glade and tried to buck. But Navvy kept his head up. With that Marc seemed to give way to ungovernable rage and plunged right through camp; he knocked over the dogs' shelter and thundered down the ridge.

Now the Navajo with the bridle in his hand was thoroughly at home. He was getting his revenge on Marc, and he would have kept his seat on a wild mustang, but Marc swerved suddenly under a low branch of a pine, sweeping the Indian off.

When Navvy did not rise we began to fear he had been seriously hurt, perhaps killed, and we ran to where he lay.

Face downward, hands outstretched, with no movement of body or muscle, he certainly appeared dead.

"Badly hurt," said Emett, "probably back broken. I have seen it before from just such accidents."

"Oh no!" cried Jones, and I felt so deeply I could not speak. Jim, who always wanted Navvy to be a dead Indian, looked profoundly sorry.

"He's a dead Indian, all right," replied Emett.

We rose from our stooping postures and stood around, uncertain and deeply grieved, until a mournful groan from Navvy afforded us much relief.

"That's your dead Indian," exclaimed Jones.

Emett stooped again and felt the Indian's back and got in reward another mournful groan.

"It's his back," said Emett, and true to his ruling passion, forever to minister to the needs of horses, men, and things, he began to rub the Indian and call for the liniment.

Jim went to fetch it, while I, still believing the Navvy to be dangerously hurt, knelt by him and pulled up his shirt, exposing the hollow of his brown back.

"Here we are," said Jim, returning on the run with the bottle.

"Pour some on," replied Emett.

Jim removed the cork and soused the liniment all over the Indian's back.

"Don't waste it," remonstrated Emett, starting to rub Navvy's back.

Then occurred a most extraordinary thing. A convulsion seemed to quiver through the Indian's body; he rose at a single leap, and uttering a wild, piercing yell broke into a run. I never saw an Indian or anybody else run so fleetly. Yell after yell pealed back to us.

Absolutely dumfounded we all gazed at each other.

"That's your dead Indian!" ejaculated Jim.

"What the hell!" exclaimed Emett, who seldom used such language.

"Look here!" cried Jones, grabbing the bottle. "See! Don't you see it?"

Jim fell face downward and began to shake.

"What?" shouted Emett and I together.

"Turpentine, you idiots! Turpentine! Jim brought the wrong bottle!"

In another second three more forms lay stretched out on the sward, and the forest rang with sounds of mirth.

VII

That night the wind switched and blew cold from
the north, and so strong that the camp-fire roared
like a furnace. "More snow" was the verdict of all
of us, and in view of this, I invited the Navajo to
share my tent.

"Sleepie-me," I said to him.

"Me savvy," he replied and forthwith proceeded
to make his bed with me.

Much to my surprise all my comrades raised
protestations, which struck me as being singularly
selfish considering they would not be inconvenienced
in any way.

"Why not?" I asked. "It's a cold night. There'll
be frost if not snow."

"Shore you'll get 'em," said Jim.

"There never was an Indian that didn't have 'em,"
added Jones.

"What?" I questioned.

They made mysterious signs that rather augmented
my ignorance as to what I might get from the Indian,
but in no wise changed my mind. When I went to
bed I had to crawl over Navvy. Moze lay at my feet
as usual and he growled so deep that I could not but
think he, too, resented the addition to my small tent.

"Mista Gay!" came in the Indian's low voice.

"Well Navvy?" I asked.

"Sleepie—sleepie?"

"Yes, Navvy, sleepy and tired. Are you?"

"Me savvy—mucha sleepie—mucha—no bueno."

I did not wonder at his feeling sleepy, tired and
bad. He did not awaken me in the morning, for

when my eyes unclosed the tent was light and he had gone. I found my companions up and doing.

We had breakfast and got into our saddles by the time the sun, a red ball low down among the pines, began to brighten and turn to gold. No snow had fallen but a thick frost encrusted the ground. The hounds, wearing cloth moccasins, which plainly they detested, trotted in front. Don showed no effects of his great run down the sliding slope after the red lioness; it was one of his remarkable qualities that he recuperated so quickly. Ranger was a little stiff, and Sounder favored his injured foot. The others were as usual.

Jones led down the big hollow to which he kept after we had passed the edge of the pines; then marking a herd of deer ahead, he turned his horse up the bank.

We breasted the ridge and jogged toward the cedar forest, which we entered without having seen the hounds show interest in anything. Under the cedars in the soft yellow dust we crossed lion tracks, many of them, but too old to carry a scent. Even North Hollow with its regular beaten runway failed to win a murmur from the pack.

"Spread out," said Jones, "and look for tracks. I'll keep the center and hold in the hounds."

Signalling occasionally to one another we crossed almost the breadth of the cedar forest to its western end, where the open sage flats inclined to the rim. In one of those flats I came upon a broken sage bush, the grass being thick thereabout. I discovered no track but dismounted and scrutinized the surroundings carefully. A heavy body had been dragged across

the sage, crushing it. The ends of broken bushes
were green, the leaves showed bruises.

I began to feel like Don when he scented game.
Leading my mustang I slowly proceeded across the
open, guided by an occasional down-trodden bush or
tuft of grass. As I neared the cedars again Foxie
snorted. Under the first tree I found a ghastly bunch
of red bones, a spread of grayish hairs and a split
skull. The bones, were yet wet; two long doe ears
were still warm. Then I saw big lion tracks in the
dust and even a well pressed imprint of a lion's body
where he had rolled or lain.

The two yells I sent ringing into the forest were
productive of interesting results. Answers came from
near and far. Then, what with my calling and the
replies, the forest rang so steadily with shrill cries
that the echoes had no chance to follow.

An elephant in the jungle could not have caused
more crashing and breaking of brush than did Emett
as he made his way to me. He arrived from the
forest just as Jim galloped across the flat. Mutely I
held up the two long ears.

"Get on your horse!" cried Jim after one quick
glance at the spread of bones and hair.

It was well he said that, for I might have been left
behind. I ran to Foxie and vaulted upon him. A flash
of yellow appeared among the sage and a string of
yelps split the air.

"It's Don!" yelled Jim.

Well we knew that. What a sight to see him
running straight for us! He passed, a savage yellow
wolf in his ferocity, and disappeared like a gleam
under the gloomy cedars.

We spurred after him. The other hounds sped by.

Jones closed in on us from the left, and in a few minutes we were strung out behind Emett, fighting the branches, dodging and swerving, hugging the saddle, and always sending out our sharp yells.

The race was furious but short. The three of us coming up together found Emett dismounted on the extreme end of West Point.

"The hounds have gone down," he said, pointing to the runway.

We all listened to the meaning bays.

"Shore they've got him up!" asserted Jim. " Like as not they found him under the rim here, sleeping off his gorge. Now fellows, I'll go down. It might be a good idea for you to spread along the rim."

With that we turned our horses eastward and rode as close to the rim as possible. Clumps of cedars and deep fissures often forced us to circle them. The hounds, traveling under the walls below, kept pace with us and then forged ahead, which fact caused Jones to dispatch Emett on the gallop for the next runway at North Hollow.

Soon Jones bade me dismount and make my way out upon one of the promontories, while he rode a little farther on. As I tied my mustang I heard the hounds, faint and far beneath. I waded through the sage and cedar to the rim.

Cape after cape jutted out over the abyss. Some were very sharp and bare, others covered with cedar; some tottering crags with a crumbling bridge leading to their rims; and some ran down like giant steps. From one of these I watched below. The slope here under the wall was like the side of a rugged mountain. Somewhere down among the dark patches of cedar and the great blocks of stone the hounds were hunting the lion, but I could not see one of them.

The promontory I had chosen had a split, and choked as this was with brush, rock, and shale, it seemed a place where I might climb down. Once started, I could not turn back, and sliding, clinging to what afforded, I worked down the crack. A wall of stone hid the sky from me part of the way. I came out a hundred feet below upon a second promontory of huge slabs of yellow stone. Over these I clambered, to sit with my feet swinging over the last one.

Straight before my gaze yawned the awful expanse of the canyon. In the soft morning light the red mesas, the yellow walls, the black domes were less harsh than in the full noonday sun, purer than in the tender shadow of twilight. Below me were slopes and slides divided by ravines full of stones as large as houses, with here and there a lonesome leaning crag, giving irresistible proof of the downward trend, of the rolling, weathering ruins of the rim. Above the wall bulged out full of fissures, ragged and rotten shelves, toppling columns of yellow limestone, beaded with quartz and colored by wild flowers wonderfully growing in crannies.

Wild and rare as was this environment, I gave it but a glance and a thought. The bay of the hounds caused me to bend sharp and eager eyes to the open spaces of stone and slide below. Luck was mine as usual; the hounds were working up toward me. How I strained my sight! Hearing a single cry I looked eastward to see Jones silhouetted against the blue on a black promontory. He seemed a giant primeval man overlooking the ruin of a former world. I signalled him to make for my point.

Black Ranger hove in sight at the top of a yellow slide. He was at fault but hunting hard. Jude and Sounder bayed off to his left. I heard Don's clear voice, permeating the thin, cool air, seemingly to leave a quality of wildness upon it; yet I could not locate him. Ranger disappeared. Then for a time I only heard Jim. Moze was next to appear and he, too, was upward bound. A jumble of stone hid him, and then Ranger again showed. Evidently he wanted to get around the bottom of a low crag, for he jumped and jumped only to fall back.

Quite naturally my eyes searched that crag. Stretched out upon the top of it was the long, slender body of a lion.

"Hi! hi! hi! hi! hi!" I yelled till my lungs failed me.

"Where are you?" came from above.

"Here! Here!" I cried seeing Jones on the rim. "Come down. Climb down the crack. The lion is here; on top of that round crag. He's fooled the hounds and they can't find him."

"I see him! I see him!" yelled Jones. Then he roared out a single call for Emett that pealed like a clear clarion along the curved broken rim wall, opening up echoes which clapped like thunder.

While Jones clattered down I turned again to the lion. He lay with head hidden under a little shelf and he moved not a muscle. What a place for him to choose! But for my accidental venturing down the broken fragments and steps of the rim he could have remained safe from pursuit.

Suddenly, right under my feet, Don opened his string of yelps. I could not see him but decided he must be above the lion on the crag. I leaned over as

far as I dared. At that moment among the varied and
thrilling sounds about me I became vaguely aware of
hard, panting breaths, like coughs somewhere in my
vicinity. As Jones had set in motion bushels of stone
and had already scraped his feet over the rocks
behind me I thought the forced respiration came
from him. When I turned he was yet far off—too far
for me to hear him breathe. I thought this circumstance strange but straightway forgot it.

On the moment from my right somewhere Don
pealed out his bugle blast, and immediately after
Sounder and Jude joining him, sent up the thrice
welcome news of a treed lion.

"There're two! There're two!" I yelled to Jones,
now working down to my right.

"He's treed down here. I've got him spotted!"
replied Jones. "You stay there and watch your lion.
Yell for Emett."

Signal after signal for Emett earned no response,
though Jim far below to the left sent me an answer.

The next few minutes, or more likely half an
hour, passed with Jones and me separated from each
other by a wall of broken stone, waiting impatiently
for Jim and Emett, while the hounds bayed one lion
and I watched the other.

Calmness was impossible under such circumstances.
No man could have gazed into that marvel of color
and distance, with wild life about him, with wild
sounds ringing in his ears, without yielding to the
throb and race of his wild blood.

Emett did not come. Jim had not answered a yell
for minutes. No doubt he needed his breath. He
came into sight just to the left of our position, and he
ran down one side of the ravine to toil up the other. I

hailed him, Jones hailed him and the hounds hailed him.

"Steer to your left, Jim!" I called. "There's a lion on that crag above you. He might jump. Round the cliff to the left—Jones is there!"

The most painful task it was for me to sit there and listen to the sound rising from below without being able to see what happened. My lion had peeped up once, and, seeing me, had crouched closer to his crag, evidently believing he was unseen, which obviously made it imperative for me to keep my seat and hold him there as long as possible.

But to hear the various exclamations thrilled me enough.

"Hyar Moze—get out of that. Catch him—hold him! Damn these rotten limbs. Hand me a pole— Jones, back down—back down! he's comin'—Hi! Hi! Whoop! Boo—o! There—now you've got him! No, no; it slipped! Now! Look out, Jim, from under— he's going to jump!"

A smashing and rattling of loose stones and a fiery burst of yelps with trumpet-like yells followed close upon Jones' last words. Then two yellow streaks leaped down the ravine. The first was the lion, the second was Don. The rest of the pack came tumbling helter-skelter in their wake. Following them raced Jim in long kangaroo leaps, with Jones in the rear, running for all he was worth. The animated and musical procession passed up out of the ravine and gradually lengthened as the lion gained and Jones lost, till it passed altogether from my jealous sight.

On the other side of the ridge of cedars the hounds treed their quarry again, as was easy to tell by their change from sharp intermittent yelping to an unbro-

ken, full, deep chorus. Then presently all quieted
down, and for long moments at a time the still
silence enfolded the slope. Shouts now and then
floated up on the wind and an occasional bark.

I sat there for an hour by my watch, though it
seemed only a few minutes, and all that time my lion
lay crouched on his crag and never moved.

I looked across the curve of the canyon to the
purple breaks of the Siwash and the shaggy side of
Buckskin Mountain and far beyond to where Kanab
Canyon opened its dark mouth, and farther still to
the Pink Cliffs of Utah, weird and dim in the distance.

Something swelled within my breast at the thought
that for the time I was part of that wild scene. The
eye of an eagle soaring above would have placed me
as well as my lion among the few living things in the
range of his all-compassing vision. Therefore, all
was mine, not merely the lion—for he was only the
means to an end—but the stupendous, unnamable
thing beneath me, this chasm that hid mountains in
the shades of its cliffs, and the granite tombs, some
gleaming pale, passionless, others red and warm,
painted by a master hand; and the windcaves, dark-
portaled under their mist curtains, and all that was
deep and far off, unapproachable, unattainable, of
beauty exceeding, dressed in ever-changing hues,
was mine by right of presence, by right of the eye to
see and the mind to keep.

"Waa-hoo!"

The cry lifted itself out of the depths. I saw Jones
on the ridge of cedars.

"All right here—have you kept your line there?"
he yelled.

"All's well—come along, come along," I replied.

I watched them coming, and all the while my lion never moved. The hounds reached the base of the cliff under me, but they could not find the lion, though they scented him, for they kept up a continual baying. Jim got up to the shelf under me and said they had tied up the lion and left him below. Jones toiled slowly up the slope.

"Some one ought to stay down there; he might jump," I called in warning.

"That crag is forty feet high on this side," he replied.

I clambered back over the uneven mass, let myself down between the boulders and crawled under a dark ridge, and finally with Jim catching my rile and camera and then lending his shoulders, I reached the bench below. Jones came puffing around a corner of the cliff, and soon all three of us with the hounds stood out on the rocky shelf with only a narrow space between us and the crouching lion.

Before we had a moment to speak, much less form a plan of attack, the lion rose, spat at us defiantly, and deliberately jumped off the crag. We heard him strike with a frightful thud.

Surprise held us dumb. To take the leap to the slope below seemed beyond any beast not endowed with wings. We saw the lion bounding down the identical trail which the other lion had taken. Jones came out of his momentary indecision.

"Hold the dogs! Call them back!" he yelled hoarsely. "They'll kill the lion we tied! They'll kill him!"

The hounds had scattered off the bench here and there, everywhere, to come together on the trail below. Already they were in full cry with the match-

less Don at the fore. Manifestly to call them back
was an injustice, as well as impossible. In ten seconds they were out of sight.

In silence we waited, each listening, each feeling
the tragedy of the situation, each praying that they
would pass by the poor, helpless, bound lion. Suddenly the regular baying swelled to a burst of savage, snarling fury, such as the pack made in a
vicious fight. This ceased—short silence ensued; Don's
sharp voice woke the echoes, then the regular baying
continued.

As with one thought, we all sat down. Painful as
the certainty was it was not so painful as that listening, hoping suspense.

"Shore they can't be blamed," said Jim finally.
"Bumping their nose into a tied lion that way—how'd
they know?"

"Who could guess the second lion would jump off
that quick and run back to our captive?" burst out
Jones.

"Shore we might have knowed it," replied Jim.
"Well, I'm goin' after the pack."

He gathered up his lasso and strode off the bench.
Jones said he would climb back to the rim, and I
followed Jim.

Why the lions ran in that particular direction was
clear to me when I saw the trail. It was a runway,
smooth and hard packed. I trudged along it with
rather less enjoyment than on any trail I had ever
followed to the canyon. Jim waited for me over the
cedar ridge and showed me where the captive lion
lay dead. The hounds had not torn him. They had
killed him and passed on after the other.

"He was a fine fellow, all of seven feet, we'll skin him on our way back."

Only dogged determination coupled with a sense of duty to the hounds kept us on that trail. For the time being enthusiasm had been submerged. But we had to follow the pack.

Jim, less weighted down and perhaps less discouraged, forged ahead up and down. The sun had burned all the morning coolness out of the air. I perspired and panted and began to grow weary. Jim's signal called me to hurry. I took to a trot and came upon him and the hounds under a small cedar. The lion stood among the dead branches. His sides were shaking convulsively and his short breaths could be plainly heard. He had the most blazing eyes and most untamed expression of any wild creature I have ever seen; and this amazed me considering I had kept him on a crag for over an hour, and had come to look upon him as my own.

"What'll we do, Jim, now that we have him treed?"

"Shore, we'll tie him up," declared Jim.

The lion stayed in the cedar long enough for me to photograph him twice, then he leaped down again and took to his back trail. We followed as fast as we could, soon to find that the hounds had put him up another cedar. From this he jumped down among the dogs, scattered them as if they had been so many leaves, and bounded up the slope out of sight.

I laid aside my rifle and camera and tried to keep up with Jim. The lion ran straight up the slope and treed again under the wall. Before we covered half the distance he was on the go once more, flying down in clouds of dust.

"Don is makin' him hump," said Jim.

And that alone was enough to spur us on. We would reward the noble hound if we had the staying power. Don and his pack ran westward this time, and along a mile of the beaten trail put him up two more trees. But these we could not see and judged only by the sound.

"Look there!" cried Jim. "Darn me if he ain't comin' right at us."

It was true. Ahead of us the lion appeared, loping wearily. We stopped in our tracks undecided. Jim drew his revolver. Once or twice the lion disappeared behind stones and cedars. When he sighted us he stopped, looked back, then again turning toward us, he left the trail to plunge down. He had barely got out of sight when old Don came pattering along the trail; then Ranger leading the others. Don did not even put his nose to the ground where the lion had switched, but leaped aside and went down. Here the long section of slope between the lion's runway and the second wall had been weathered and worn, racked and convulsed into deep ravines, with ridges between. We climbed and fell and toiled on, always with the bay of the hounds in our ears. We leaped fissures, we loosened avalanches, rolling them to crash and roar below, and send long, rumbling echoes out into the canyon.

A gorge in the yellow rock opened suddenly before us. We stood at the constricted neck of one of the great splits in the second wall. The side opposite was almost perpendicular, and formed of mass on mass of broken stones. This was a weathered slope on a gigantic scale. Points of cliffs jutted out; caves and cracks lined the wall.

"This is a rough place," said Jim; "but a lion could get over the second wall here, an' I believe a man could too. The hounds seemed to be back further toward where the split narrows."

Through densely massed cedars and thickets of prickly thorns we wormed our way to come out at the neck of the gorge.

"There ye are!" sang out Jim. The hounds were all on a flat shelf some few feet below us, and on a sharp point of rock close by, but too far for the dogs to reach, crouched the lion. He was gasping and frothing at the mouth.

"Shore if he'd only stay there—" said Jim.

He loosened his lasso, and stationing himself just above the tired beast he prepared to cast down the loop. The first throw failed of its purpose, but the rope hit the lion. He got up painfully it seemed, and faced the dogs. That way barred he turned to the cliff. Almost opposite him a shelf leaned out. He looked at it, then paced to and fro like a beast in a cage.

He looked again at the hounds, then up at us, all around, and finally concentrated his attention on the shelf; his long length sagged in the middle, he stretched low, his muscles gathered and strung, and he sprang like a tawny streak.

His aim was true, the whole forepart of his body landed on the shelf and he hung there. Then he slipped. We distinctly heard his claws scrape the hard, smooth rock. He fell, turning a somersault, struck twenty feet below on the rough slant, bounded from that to fall down, striking suddenly and then to roll, a yellow wheel that lodged behind a rock and stretched out to move no more.

The hounds were silent; Jim and I were silent; a few little stones rattled, then were still. The dead silence of the canyon seemed to pay tribute to the lion's unquenchable spirit and to the freedom he had earned to the last.

VIII

How long Jim and I sat there we never knew. The second tragedy, not so pitiful but as heart sickening as the first, crushed our spirits.

"Shore he was a game lion," said Jim. "An' I'll have to get his skin."

"I'm all in, Jim. I couldn't climb out of that hole." I said.

"You needn't. Rest a little, take a good drink an' leave your canteen here for me; then get your things back there on the trail an' climb out. We're not far from West Point. I'll go back after the first lion's skin an' then climb straight up. You lead my horse to the point where you came off the rim."

He clattered along the gorge knocking the stones and started down. I watched him letting himself over the end of the huge slabs until he passed out of my sight. A good, long drink revived me and I began the ascent.

From that moment on time did not matter to me. I forgot all about it. I felt only my leaden feet and my laboring chest and dripping skin. I did not even notice the additional weight of my rifle and camera though they must have overburdened me. I kept my eyes on the lion runway and plunged away with short steps. To look at these towering walls would have been to surrender.

At last, stumbling, bursting, sick, I gained the rim and had to rest before I could mount. When I did get into the saddle I almost fell from it.

Jones and Emett were waiting for me at the promontory where I had tied my horse, and were soon acquainted with the particulars of my adventure, and that Jim would probably not get out for hours. We made tracks for camp, and never did a place rouse in me such a sense of gratefulness. Emett got dinner and left on the fire a kettle of potato stew for Jim. It was almost dark when that worthy came riding into camp. We never said a word as he threw the two lion skins on the ground.

"Fellows, you shore have missed the wind-up!" he exclaimed.

We all looked at him and he looked at us.

"Was there any more?" I asked weakly.

"Shore! An' it beats hell! When I got the skin of the lion the dogs killed I started to work up to the place I knowed you'd leave my horse. It's bad climbing where you came down. I got on the side of that cliff an' saw where I could work out, if I could climb a smooth place. So I tried. There was little cracks an' ridges for my feet and hands. All to once, just above where I helped you down, I heard a growl. Looking up I saw a big lion, bigger'n any we chased except Sultan, an' he was pokin' his head out of a hole, an' shore telling me to come no further. I couldn't let go with either hand to reach my gun, because I'd have fallen, so I yelled at him with all my might. He spit at me an' then walked out of the hole over the bench as proud as a lord an' jumped down where I couldn't see him any more. I climbed out all right but he'd gone. An' I'll tell you for a minute, he shore made me sweat.''

"By George!" I yelled, greatly excited. "I heard that lion breathing. Don chased him up there. I heard hard, wheezing breaths somewhere behind me, but in the excitement I didn't pay any attention to them. I thought it was Jones panting, but now I know what it meant.''

"Shore. He was there all the time, lookin' at you an' maybe he could have reached you.''

We were all too exhausted for more discussion and putting that off until the next day we sought our beds. It was hardly any wonder that I felt myself jumping even in my sleep, and started up wildly more than once in the dead of night.

Morning found us all rather subdued, yet more inclined to a philosophical resignation as regarded the difficulties of our special kind of hunting. Capturing the lions on the level of the plateau was easy compared to following them down into canyons and bringing them up alone. We all agreed that that was next to impossible. Another feature, which before we had not considered, added to our perplexity and it was a dawning consciousness that we would be perhaps less cruel if we killed the lions outright. Jones and Emett arrayed themselves on the side that life even in captivity was preferable; while Jim and I, no doubt still under the poignant influence of the last lion's heroic race and end, inclined to freedom or death. We compromised on the reasonable fact that as yet we had shown only a jackass kind of intelligence.

About eleven o'clock while the others had deserted camp temporarily for some reason or other, I was lounging upon an odorous bed of pine needles. The sun shone warmly, the sky gleamed bright azure through the openings of the great trees, a dry west breeze murmured through the forest. I was lying on my bed musing idly and watching a yellow wood-pecker when suddenly I felt a severe bite on my shoulder. I imagined an ant had bitten me through my shirt. In a moment or so afterward I received, this time on my breast, another bite that left no room for imagination. There was some kind of an animal inside my shirt, and one that made a mosquito, black-fly, or flea seem tame.

Suddenly a thought swept on the heels of my indolent and rather annoying realization. Could I have gotten from the Navajo what Jim and Jones so characteristically called " 'em"? I turned cold all over. And on the very instant I received another bite that burned like fire.

The return of my companions prevented any open demonstration of my fears and condition of mind, but I certainly swore inwardly. During the dinner hour I felt all the time as if I had on a horsehair shirt with the ends protruding toward my skin, and, in the exaggerated sensitiveness of the moment, made sure " 'em" were chasing up and down my back.

After dinner I sneaked off into the woods. I remembered that Emett had said there was only one way to get rid of " 'em," and that was to disrobe and make a microscopical search of garments and person. With serious mind and murderous intent I undressed. In the middle of the back of my jersey I discovered several long, uncanny, gray things.

"I guess I got 'em," I said gravely.

Then I sat on a pine log in a state of unadorned

nature, oblivious to all around, intent only on the massacre of the things that had violated me. How much time flew I could not guess. Great loud "Hawhaws!" roused me to consternation. There behind me stood Jones and Emett shaking as if with the ague.

"It's not funny!" I shouted in a rage. I had the unreasonable suspicion that they had followed me to see my humiliation. Jones, who cracked a smile about as often as the equinoxes came, and Emett the sober Mormon, laughed until they cried.

"I was—just wondering—what your folks would—think—if they—saw you—now," gurgled Jones.

That brought to me the humor of the thing, and I joined in their mirth.

"All I hope is that you fellows will get ''em' too," I said.

"The Good Lord preserve me from that particular breed of Navvy's," cried Emett.

Jones wriggled all over at the mere suggestion. Now so much from the old plainsman, who had confessed to intimate relations with every creeping, crawling thing in the West, attested powerfully to the unforgettable singularity of what I got from Navvy.

I returned to camp determined to make the best of the situation, which owing to my failure to catch all of the gray devils, remained practically unchanged. Jim had been acquainted with my dilemma, as was manifest in his wet eyes and broad grin with which he greeted me.

"I think I'd scalp the Navvy," he said.

"You make the Indian sleep outside after this, snow or no snow," was Jones' suggestion.

"No I won't; I won't show a yellow streak like that. Besides, I want to give 'em to you fellows."

A blank silence followed my statement, to which Jim replied:

"Shore that'll be easy; Jones'll have 'em, so'll Emett, an' by thunder I'm scratchin' now."

"Navvy, look here," I said severely, "mucha no bueno! heap bad! You—me!" here I scratched myself and made signs that a wooden Indian would have understood.

"Me savvy," he replied, sullenly, then flared up. "Heap big lie."

He turned on his heel, erect, dignified, and walked away amid the roars of my gleeful comrades.

IX

One by one my companions sought their blankets, leaving the shadows, the dying embers, the slow-rising moan of the night wind to me. Old Moze got up from among the other hounds and limped into my tent, where I heard him groan as he lay down. Don, Sounder, and Ranger were fast asleep in well-earned rest. Shep, one of the pups, whined and impatiently tossed his short chain. Remembering that he had not been loose all day, I unbuckled his collar and let him go.

He licked my hand, stretched and shook himself, lifted his shapely, sleek head and sniffed the wind. He trotted around the circle cast by the fire and looked out into the darkening shadows. It was plain that Shep's instincts were developing fast; he was ambitious to hunt. But sure in my belief that he was afraid of the black night and would stay in camp, I went to bed.

The Navajo who slept with me snored serenely and Moze growled in his dreams; the wind swept through the pines with an intermittent rush. Some time in the after part of the night I heard a distant sound. Remote, mournful, wild, it sent a chill creeping over me. Borne faintly to my ears, it was a fit accompaniment to the moan of the wind in the pines. It was not the cry of a trailing wolf, nor the lonesome howl of a prowling coyote, nor the strange, low sound, like a cough, of a hunting cougar, though it had a semblance of all three. It was the bay of a hound, thinned out by distance, and it served to keep me wide awake. But for a while, what with the roar and swell of the wind and Navvy's snores, I could hear it only at long intervals.

Still, in the course of an hour, I followed the sound, or imagined so, from a point straight in line with my feet to one at right angles with my head. Finally deciding it came from Shep, and fancying he was trailing a deer or coyote, I tried to go to sleep again.

In this I would have succeeded had not, all at once, our captive lions begun to growl. That ominous, low murmuring awoke me with a vengeance, for it was unusual for them to growl in the middle of the night. I wondered if they, as well as the pup, had gotten the scent of a prowling lion.

I reached down to my feet and groped in the dark for Moze. Finding him, I gave him a shake. The old gladiator groaned, stirred, and came out of what must have been dreams of hunting meat. He slapped his tail against my bed. As luck would have it, just then the wind abated to a soft moan, and clear and sharp came the bay of a hound. Moze heard it, for he stopped wagging his tail, his body grew tense under my hand, and he vented his low, deep grumble.

I lay there undecided. To wake my companions was hardly to be considered, and to venture off into the forest alone, where old Sultan might be scouting, was not exactly to my taste. And trying to think what to do, and listening for the bay of the pup, and hearing mostly the lions growling and the wind roaring, I fell asleep.

"Hey! are you ever going to get up?" some one yelled into my drowsy brain. I roused and opened my eyes. The yellow, flickering shadows on the wall of my tent told me that the sun had long risen. I found my companions finishing breakfast. The first thing I did was to look over the dogs. Shep, the black-and-white pup, was missing.

"Where's Shep?" I asked.

"Shore, I ain't seen him this mornin'," replied Jim.

Thereupon I told what I had heard during the night.

"Everybody listen," said Jones.

We quieted down and sat like statues. A gentle, cool breeze, barely moving the pine tips, had succeeded the night wind. The sound of horses munching their oats, and an occasional clink, rattle, and growl from the lions did not drown the faint but unmistakable yelps of a pup.

"South, toward the canyon," said Jim, as Jones got up.

"Now, it'd be funny if that little Shep, just to get even with me for tying him up so often, has treed a lion all by himself,'' commented Jones. ''And I'll bet that's just what he's done.''

He called the hounds about him and hurried westward through the forest.

''Shore, it might be.'' Jim shook his head knowingly. ''I reckon it's only a rabbit, but anythin' might happen in this place.''

I finished breakfast and went into my tent for something—I forget what, for wild yells from Emett and Jim brought me flying out again.

''Listen to that!'' cried Jim, pointing west.

The hounds had opened up; their full, wild chorus floated clearly on the breeze, and above it Jones' stentorian yell signaled us.

''Shore, the old man can yell,'' continued Jim. ''Grab your lassos an' hump yourselves. I've got the collar an' chain.''

''Come on, Navvy,'' shouted Emett. He grasped the Indian's wrist and started to run, jerking Navvy into the air at every jump. I caught up my camera and followed. We crossed two shallow hollows, and then saw the hounds and Jones among the pines not far ahead.

In my excitement I outran my companions and dashed into an open glade. First I saw Jones waving his long arms; next the dogs, noses upward, and Don actually standing on his hind legs; then a dead pine with a wellknown tawny shape outlined against the blue sky.

''Hurrah for Shep!'' I yelled, and right vigorously did my comrades join in.

''It's another female,'' said Jones, when we calmed down, ''and fair sized. That's the best tree for our purpose that I ever saw a lion in. So spread out, boys; surround her and keep noisy.''

Navvy broke from Emett at this juncture and ran away. But evidently overcome by curiosity, he stopped to hide behind a bush, from which I saw his black head protruding.

When Jones swung himself on the first stubby branch of the pine, the lioness, some fifteen feet above, leaped to another limb, and the one she had left cracked, swayed, and broke. It fell directly upon Jones, the blunt end striking his head and knocking him out of the tree. Fortunately, he landed on his feet; otherwise there would surely have been bones broken. He appeared stunned, and reeled so that Emett caught him. The blood poured from a wound in his head.

This sudden shock sobered us instantly. On examination we found a long, jagged cut in Jones' scalp. We bathed it with water from my canteen and with snow Jim procured from a nearby hollow, eventually stopping the bleeding. I insisted on Jones coming to camp to have the wound properly dressed, and he insisted on having it bound with a bandana; after which he informed us that he was going to climb the tree again.

We objected to this. Each of us declared his willingness to go up and rope the lion; but Jones would not hear of it.

"I'm not doubting your courage," he said. "It's only that you cannot tell what move the lion would make next, and that's the danger."

We could not gainsay this, and as not one of us wanted to kill the animal or let her go, Jones had his way. So he went up the tree, passed the first branch and then another. The lioness changed her position, growled, spat, clawed the twigs, tried to keep the tree trunk between her and Jones, and at length got out on a branch in a most favorable position for roping.

The first cast of the lasso did the business, and Jim and Emett with nimble fingers tied up the hounds.

"Coming," shouted Jones. He slid down, hand over hand, on the rope, the lioness holding his weight with apparent ease.

"Make your noose ready," he yelled to Emett.

I had to drop my camera to help Jones and Jim pull the animal from her perch. The branches broke in a shower; then the lioness, hissing, snarling, whirling, plunged down. She nearly jerked the rope out of our hands, but we lowered her to Emett, who noosed her hind paws in a flash.

"Make fast your rope," shouted Jones. "There, that's good! Now let her down—easy."

As soon as the lioness touched ground we let go the lasso, which whipped up and over the branch. She became a round, yellow, rapidly moving ball. Emett was the first to catch the loose lasso, and he checked the rolling cougar. Jones leaped to assist him and the two of them straightened out the struggling animal, while Jim swung another noose at her. On the second throw he caught a front paw.

"Pull hard! Stretch her out!" yelled Jones. He grasped a stout piece of wood and pushed it at the lioness. She caught it in her mouth, making the splinters fly. Jones shoved her head back on the ground and pressed his brawny knee on the bar of wood.

"The collar! The collar! Quick!" he called.

I threw chain and collar to him, which in a moment he had buckled round her neck.

"There, we've got her!" he said. "It's only a short way over to camp, so we'll drag her without muzzling."

As he rose the lioness lurched, and reaching him, fastened her fangs in his leg. Jones roared. Emett and Jim yelled. And I, though frightened, was so obsessed with the idea of getting a picture that I began to fumble with the shutter of my camera.

"Grab the chain! Pull her off!" bawled Jones.

I ran in, took up the chain with both hands, and tugged with all my might. Emett, too, had all his weight on the lasso round her neck. Between the two of us we choked her hold loose, but she brought Jones' leather leggin in her teeth. Then I dropped the chain and jumped.

"**__ __ **__ __!" exploded Jones to me. "Do you think more of a picture than of saving my life?" Having expressed this not unreasonable protest, he untied the lasso that Emett had made fast to a small sapling.

Then the three men, forming points of a triangle around an animated center, began a march through the forest that for variety of action and splendid vociferation beat any show I ever beheld.

So rare was it that the Navajo came out of his retreat and, straightway forgetting his reverence and fear, began to execute a ghost-dance, or war-dance, or at any rate some kind of an Indian dance, along the side lines.

There were moments when the lioness had Jim and Jones on the ground and Emett wobbling; others when she ran on her bound legs and chased the two in front and dragged the one behind; others when she came within an ace of getting her teeth in somebody.

They had caught a Tartar. They dared not let her go, and though Jones evidently ordered it, no one made fast his rope to a tree. There was no opportunity. She was in the air three parts of the time and the fourth she was invisible for dust. The lassos were each thirty feet long, but even with that the men could just barely keep out of her reach.

Then came the climax, as it always comes in a lion hunt, unerringly, unexpectedly, and with lightning swiftness. The three men were nearing the bottom of the second hollow, well spread out, lassos taut, facing one another. Jones stumbled and the lioness leaped his way. The weight of both brought Jim over, sliding and slipping, with his rope slackening. The leap of the lioness carried her within reach of Jones; and as he raised himself, back toward her, she reached a big paw for him just as Emett threw all his bull strength and bulk on his lasso.

The seat of Jones' trousers came away with the lioness' claws. Then she fell backward, overcome by Emett's desperate lunge. Jones sprang up with the velocity of an Arab tumbler, and his scarlet face, working spasmodically, and his moving lips, showed how utterly unable he was to give expression to his rage. I had a stitch in my side that nearly killed me, but laugh I had to though I should die for it.

No laughing matter was it for them. They volleyed and thundered back and forth meaningless words of which "hell" was the only one distinguishable, and probably the word that best described their situation.

All the while, however, they had been running

from the lioness, which brought them before they realized it right into camp. Our captive lions cut up fearfully at the hubbub, and the horses stampeded in terror.

"Whoa!" yelled Jones, whether to his companions or to the struggling cougar, no one knew. But Navvy thought Jones addressed the cougar.

"Whoa!" repeated Navvy. "No savvy whoa! No savvy whoa!" which proved conclusively that the Navajo had understanding as well as wit.

Soon we had another captive safely chained and growling away in tune with the others. I went back to untie the hounds, to find them sulky and out of sorts from being so unceremoniously treated. They noisily trailed the lioness into camp, where, finding her chained, they formed a ring around her.

Thereafter the day passed in round-the-camp-fire chat and task. For once Jim looked at Navvy with toleration. We dressed the wound in Jones' head and laughed at the condition of his trousers and at his awkward attempts to piece them.

"Mucha dam cougie," remarked Navvy. "No savvy whoa!"

The lions growled all day. And Jones kept repeating: "To think how Shep fooled me!"

X

Next morning Jones was out bright and early, yelling at Navvy to hurry with the horses, calling to the hounds and lions, just as usual.

Navvy had finally come to his full share of praise from all of us. Even Jim acknowledged that the Indian was invaluable to a hunting party in a country where grass and water were hard to find and wild horses haunted the trails.

"*Tohodena! Tohodena!* (hurry! hurry!)" said Navvy, mimicking Jones that morning.

As we sat down to breakfast he loped off into the forest and before we got up the bells of the horses were jingling in the hollow.

"I believe it's going to be cloudy," said Jones, "and if so we can hunt all day."

We rode down the ridge to the left of Middle Canyon, and had trouble with the hounds all the way. First they ran foul of a coyote, which was the one and only beast they could not resist. Spreading out to head them off, we separated. I cut into a hollow and rode to its head, where I went up. I heard the hounds and presently saw a big, white coyote making fast time through the forest glades. It looked as if he would cross close in front of me, so I pulled Foxie to a standstill, jumped off and knelt with my rifle ready. But the sharp-eyed coyote saw my horse and shied off. I had not much hope to hit him so far away, and the five bullets I sent after him, singing and zipping, served only to make him run faster. I mounted Foxie and intercepted the hounds coming up sharply on the trail, and turned them toward my companions, now hallooing from the ridge below.

Then the pack lost a good hour on several lion tracks that were a day old, and for such trails we had no time. We reached the cedars however at seven o'clock, and as the sky was overcast with low dun-colored clouds and the air cool, we were sure it was not too late.

One of the capes of the plateau between Middle

and Left Canyon was a narrow strip of rock, covered with a dense cedar growth and cut up into smaller canyons, all running down inevitably toward the great canyon. With but a single bark to warn us, Don got out of our sight and hearing; and while we split to look and call for him the remainder of the pack found the lion trail that he had gone on, and they left us trying to find a way out as well as to find each other. I kept the hounds in hearing for some time and meanwhile I signalled to Emett who was on my right flank. Jones and Jim might as well have vanished off the globe for all I could see or hear of them. A deep, narrow gully into which I had to lead Foxie and carefully coax him out took so much time that when I once more reached a level I could not hear the hounds or get an answer to my signal cry.

"Waa-hoo!" I called again.

Away on the dry rarified air pealed the cry, piercing the cedar forest, splitting sharp in the vaulted canyons, rolling loud and long, to lose power, to die away in muffling echo. But the silence returned no answer.

I rode on under the cedars, through a dark, gloomy forest, silent, almost spectral, which brought irresistibly to my mind the words "I found me in a gloomy wood astray." I was lost though I knew the direction of the camp. This section of cedar forest was all but impenetrable. Dead cedars were massed in gray tangles, live cedars, branches touching the ground, grew close together. In this labyrinth I lost my bearings. I turned and turned, crossed my own back trail, which in desperation I followed, coming out of the cedars at the deep and narrow canyon.

Here I fired my revolver. The echo boomed out

like the report of heavy artillery, but no answering
shot rewarded me. There was no alternative save to
wander along the canyon and through the cedars
until I found my companions. This I began to do,
disgusted with my awkwardness in losing them. Turning Foxie westward I had scarcely gotten under way
when Don came trotting toward me.

"Hello, old boy!" I called. Don appeared as happy
to see me as I was to see him. He flopped down on
the ground; his dripping tongue rolled as he panted;
covered with dust and flecked with light froth he
surely looked to be a tired hound.

"All in, eh Don!" I said dismounting. "Well,
we'll rest awhile." Then I discovered blood on his
nose, which I found to have come from a deep
scratch. "A—ah! been pushing a lion too hard this
morning? Got your nose scratched, didn't you? You
great, crazy hound, don't you know some day you'll
chase your last lion?"

Don wagged his tail as if to say he knew it all
very well. I wet my handkerchief from my canteen
and started to wash the blood and dust from his
nose, when he whined and licked my fingers.

"Thirsty?" I asked, sitting down beside him. Dent-
ing the top of my hat I poured in as much water as it
would hold and gave him to drink. Four times he
emptied my improvised cup before he was satisfied.
Then with a sigh of relief he lay down again.

The three of us rested there for perhaps half an
hour, Don and I sitting quietly on the wall of the
canyon, while Foxie browsed on occasional tufts of
grass. During that time the hound never raised his
sleek, dark head, which showed conclusively the
nature of the silence. And now that I had company—as

good company as any hunter ever had—I was once more contented.

Don got up, at length of his own volition and with a wag of his tail set off westward along the rim. Remounting my mustang I kept as close to Don's heels as the rough going permitted. The hound, however, showed no disposition to hurry, and I let him have his way without a word.

We came out in the notch of the great amphitheater or curve we had named the Bay, and I saw again the downward slope, the bold steps, the color and depth below.

I was just about to yell a signal cry when I saw Don, with hair rising stiff, run forward. He took a dozen jumps, then yelping broke down the steep, yellow and green gorge. He disappeared before I knew what had happened.

Shortly I found a lion track, freshly made, leading down. I believed I could follow wherever Don led, so I decided to go after him. I tied Foxie securely, removed my coat, kicked off spurs and chaps, and remembering past unnecessary toil, fastened a red bandana to the top of a dead snag to show me where to come up on my way out. Then I carefully strapped my canteen and camera on my back, made doubly secure my revolver, put on my heavy gloves, and started down. And I realized at once that only so lightly encumbered should I have ever ventured down the slope.

Little benches of rock, grassy on top, with here and there cedar trees, led steeply down for perhaps five hundred feet. A precipice stopped me. From it I heard Don baying below, and almost instantly saw the yellow gleam of a lion in a tree-top.

"Hi! Hi! Hi! Hi! Hi!" I yelled in wild encouragement.

I felt it would be wise to look before I leaped. The Bay lay under me, a mile wide where it opened into the great slumbering smoky canyon. All below was chaos of splintered stone and slope, green jumble of cedar, ruined, detached, sliding, standing cliff walls, leaning yellow crags—an awful hole. But I could get down, and that was all I cared for. I ran along to the left, jumping cracks, bounding over the uneven stones with sure, swift feet, and came to where the cliff ended in weathered slope and scaly bench.

It was like a game, going down that canyon. My heavy nailed boots struck fire from the rocks. My heavy gloves protected my hands as I slid and hung on and let go. I outfooted the avalanches and wherever I came to a scaly slope or bank or decayed rock, I leaped down in sheer delight.

But all too soon my progress was barred; once under the cliff I found only a gradual slope and many obstacles to go round or surmount. Luck favored me, for I ran across a runway and keeping to it made better time. I heard Don long before I tried to see him, and yelled at intervals to let him know I was coming. A white bank of weathered stones led down to a clump of cedars from where Don's bay came spurring me to greater efforts. I flew down this bank, and through an opening saw the hound standing with fore feet against a cedar. The branches over him swayed, and I saw an indistinct, tawny form move downward in the air. Then succeeded the crash and rattle of stones. Don left the tree and disappeared.

I dashed down, dodged under the cedars, threaded a maze of rocks, to find myself in a ravine with a bare, water-worn floor. In patches of sand showed the fresh tracks of Don and the lion. Running down this dry, clean bed was the easiest going I ever found in the canyon. Every rod the course jumped in a fall from four to ten feet, often more, and these I slid down. How I ever kept Don in hearing was a marvel, but still I did.

The lion evidently had no further intention of taking to a tree. From the size of his track I concluded he was old and I feared every moment to hear the sounds of a fight. Jones had said that nearly always in the case of one hound chasing an old lion, the lion would lie in wait for him and kill him. And I was afraid for Don.

Down, down, down, we went, till the yellow rim above seemed a thin band of gold. I saw that we were almost to the canyon proper, and I wondered what would happen when we reached it. The dark shaded watercourse suddenly shot out into bright light and ended in a deep cove, with perpendicular walls fifty feet high. I could see where a few rods farther on this cove opened into a huge, airy, colored canyon.

I called the hound, wondering if he had gone to the right or left of the cove. His bay answered me coming from the cedars far to the right. I turned with all the speed left in me, for I felt the chase nearing an end. Tracks of hound and lion once more showed in the dust. The slope was steep and stones I sent rolling cracked down below. Soon I had a cliff above me and had to go slow and cautiously. A misstep or slide would have precipitated me into the cove.

Almost before I knew what I was about, I stood

gasping on the gigantic second wall of the canyon, with nothing but thin air under me, except, far below, faint and indistinct purple clefts, red ridges, dotted slopes, running down to merge in a dark, winding strip of water, that was the Rio Colorado. A sullen murmur soared out of the abyss.

The coloring of my mood changed. Never had the canyon struck me so terribly with its illimitable space, its dread depth, its unscalable cliffs, and particularly with the desolate, forbidding quality of its silence.

I heard Don bark. Turning the corner of the cliff wall I saw him on a narrow shelf. He was coming toward me and when he reached me he faced again to the wall and barked fiercely. The hair on his neck bristled. I knew he did not fancy that narrow strip of rock, nor did I. But a sudden, grim, cold something had taken possession of me, and I stepped forward.

"Come on, Don, old fellow, we've got him corralled."

That was the first instance I ever knew of Don's hesitation in the chase of a lion. I had to coax him to me. But once started he took the lead and I closely followed.

The shelf was twenty feet wide and upon it close to the wall, in the dust, were the deep imprints of the lion. A jutting corner of cliff wall hid my view. I peeped around it. The shelf narrowed on the other side to a yard in width, and climbed gradually by broken steps. Don passed the corner, looked back to see if I was coming and went on. He did this four times, once even stopping to wait for me.

"I'm with you Don!" I grimly muttered. "We'll see this trail out to a finish."

I had now no eyes for the wonders of the place,

though I could not but see as I bent a piercing gaze
ahead the ponderous overhanging wall above, and
sense the bottomless depth below. I felt rather than
saw the canyon swallows, sweeping by in darting
flight, with soft rustle of wings, and I heard the
shrill chirp of some strange cliff inhabitant.

Don ceased barking. How strange that seemed to
me! We were no longer man and hound, but companions, brothers, each one relying on the other. A
protruding corner shut us from sight of what was
beyond. Don slipped around. I had to go sidewise
and shuddered as my fingers bit into the wall.

To my surprise I soon found myself on the floor
of a shallow wind cave. The lion trail led straight
across it and on. Shelves of rock stuck out above
under which I hurriedly walked. I came upon a shrub
cedar growing in a niche and marveled to see it
there. Don went slower and slower.

We suddenly rounded a point, to see the lion lying
in a box-like space in the wall. The shelf ended
there. I had once before been confronted with a like
situation, and had expected to find it here, so was
not frightened. The lion looked up from his task of
licking a bloody paw, and uttered a fierce growl. His
tail began to lash to and fro; it knocked the little
stones off the shelf. I heard them click on the wall.
Again and again he spat, showing great, white fangs.
He was a Tom, heavy and large.

It had been my purpose, of course, to photograph
this lion, and now that we had cornered him I pro-
posed to do it. What would follow had only hazily
formed in my mind, but the nucleus of it was that he
should go free. I got my camera, opened it, and
focused from between twenty and twenty-five feet.

Then a growl from Don and roar from the lion bade me come to my senses. I did so and my first movement after seeing the lion had risen threateningly was to whip out my revolver.

The lion's cruel yellow eyes darkened and darkened. In an instant I saw my error. Jones had always said in case any one of us had to face a lion, never for a single instant to shift his glance. I had forgotten that, and in that short interval when I focused my camera the lion had seen I meant him no harm, or feared him, and he had risen. Even then in desperate lessening ambition for a great picture I attempted to take one, still keeping my glance on him.

It was then that the appalling nature of my predicament made itself plain to me. The lion leaped ten feet and stood snarling horribly right in my face.

Brave, noble Don, with infinitely more sense and courage than I possessed, faced the lion and bayed him in his teeth. I raised the revolver and aimed twice, each time lowering it because I feared to shoot in such a precarious position. To wound the lion would be the worst thing I could do, and I knew that only a shot through the brain would kill him in his tracks.

"Hold him, Don, hold him!" I yelled, and I took a backward step. The lion put forward one big paw, his eyes now all purple blaze. I backed again and he came forward. Don gave ground slowly. Once the lion flashed a yellow paw at him. It was frightful to see the wide-spread claws.

In the consternation of the moment I allowed the lion to back me across the front of the wind cave, where I saw, the moment it was too late, I should have taken advantage of more space to shoot him.

Fright succeeded consternation, and I began to tremble. The lion was master of the situation. What would happen when I came to the narrow point on the shelf where it would be impossible for me to back around? I almost fainted. The thought of heroic Don saved me, and the weak moment passed.

"By God, Don, you've got the nerve, and I must have it too!"

I stopped in my tracks. The lion, appearing huge now, took slow catlike steps toward me, backing Don almost against my knees. He was so close I smelt him. His wonderful eyes, clear blue fire circled by yellow flame, fascinated me. Hugging the wall with my body I brought the revolver up, short armed, and with clinched teeth, and nerve strained to the breaking point, I aimed between the eyes and pulled the trigger.

The left eye seemed to go out blankly, then followed the bellow of the revolver and the smell of powder. The lion uttered a sound that was a mingling of snarls, howls and roars and he rose straight up, towering high over my head, beating the wall heavily with his paws.

In helpless terror I stood there forgetting weapon, fearing only the beast would fall over on me.

But in death agony he bounded out from the wall to fall into space.

I sank down on the shelf, legs powerless, body in cold sweat. As I waited, slowly my mind freed itself from a tight iron band and a sickening relief filled my soul. Tensely I waited and listened. Don whined once.

Would the lion never strike? What seemed a long

period of time ended in a low, distant roar of sliding rock, quickly dying into the solemn stillness of the canyon.

XI

I lay there for some moments slowly recovering, eyes on the far distant escarpments, now darkly red and repellent to me. When I got up my legs were still shaky and I had the strange, weak sensation of a long bedridden invalid. Three attempts were necessary before I could trust myself on the narrow strip of shelf. But once around it with the peril passed, I braced up and soon reached the turn in the wall.

After that the ascent out of the Bay was only a matter of work, which I gave with a will. Don did not evince any desire for more hunting that day. We reached the rim together, and after a short rest, I mounted my horse, and we turned for camp.

The sun had long slanted toward the western horizon when I saw the blue smoke of our camp-fire among the pines. The hounds rose up and barked as Don trotted in to the blaze, and my companions just sitting to a dinner, gave me a noisy greeting.

"Shore, we'd began to get worried," said Jim. "We all had it comin' to us to-day, and don't you forget that."

Dinner lasted for a long hour. Besides being half famished we all took time between bites to talk. I told my story first, expecting my friends to be overwhelmed, but they were not.

"It's been the greatest day of lion hunting that I ever experienced," declared Jones. "We ran bang into a nest of lions and they split. We all split and the hounds split. That tells the tale. We have nothing to show for our day's toil. Six lions chased, rounded up, treed, holed, and one lion killed, and we haven't even his skin to show. I did not go down but I helped Ranger and two of the pups chase a lion all over the lower end of the plateau. We treed him twice and I yelled for you fellows till my voice was gone."

"Well," said Emett, "I fell in with Sounder and Jude. They were hot on a trail which in a mile or two turned up this way. I came on them just at the edge of the pines where they had treed their game. I sat under that pine tree for five hours, fired all my shots to make you fellows come, yelled myself hoarse and then tried to tie up the lion alone. He jumped out and ran over the rim, where neither I nor the dogs could follow."

"Shore, I win, three of a kind," drawled Jim, as he got his pipe and carefully dusted the bowl. "When the stampede came, I got my hands on Moze and held him. I held Moze because just as the other hounds broke loose over to my right, I saw down into a little pocket where a fresh-killed deer lay half eaten. So I went down. I found two other carcasses layin' there, fresh killed last night, flesh all gone, hide gone, bones crushed, skull split open. An' damn me fellows, if that little pocket wasn't all torn to pieces. The sage was crushed flat. The ground dug up, dead snags broken, and blood and hair everywhere. Lion tracks like leaves, and old Sultan's was there. I let Moze loose and he humped the trail of several lions south over the rim. Major got down first an' came back with his tail between his legs. Moze went down and I kept close to him. It wasn't

far down, but steep and rocky, full of holes. Moze
took the trail to a dark cave. I saw the tracks of three
lions goin' in. Then I collared Moze an' waited for
you fellows. I waited there all day, an' nobody came
to my call. Then I made for camp.''

"How do you account for the torn-up appearance
of the place where you found the carcasses?'' I
asked.

"Lion fight sure,'' replied Jones. "Maybe old
Sultan ran across the three lions feeding, and pitched
into them. Such fights were common among the
lions in Yellowstone Park when I was there.''

"What chance have we to find those three lions in
a cave where Jim chased them?''

"We stand a good chance,'' said Jones. "Especially if it storms to-night.''

"Shore the snow storm is comin','', returned Jim.
Darkness clapped down on us suddenly, and the
wind roared in the pines like a mighty river tearing
its way down a rocky pass. As we could not control
the campfire, sparks of which blew fiercely, we
extinguished it and went to bed. I had just settled
myself comfortably to be sung to sleep by the concert in the pines, when Jones hailed me.

"Say, what do you think?'' he yelled, when I had
answered him. "Emett is mad. He's scratching to
beat the band. He's got 'em.''

I signalled his information with a loud whoop of
victory.

"You next, Jones! They're coming to you!''

I heard him grumble over my happy anticipation.
Jim laughed and so did the Navajo, which made me
suspect that he could understand more English than
he wanted us to suppose.

Next morning a merry yell disturbed my slumbers.
"Snowed in—snowed in!"

"Mucha snow—discass—no cougie—dam no bueno!" exclaimed Navvy.

When I peeped out to see the forest in the throes of a blinding blizzard, the great pines only pale, grotesque shadows, everything white mantled in a foot of snow, I emphasized the Indian words in straight English.

"Much snow—cold—no cougar—bad!"

"Stay in bed," yelled Jones.

"All right," I replied. "Say Jones, have you got 'em yet?"

He vouchsafed me no answer. I went to sleep then and dozed off and on till noon, when the storm abated. We had dinner, or rather breakfast, round a blazing bonfire.

"It's going to clear up," said Jim.

The forest around us was a somber and gloomy place. The cloud that had enveloped the plateau lifted and began to move. It hit the tree tops, sometimes rolling almost to the ground, then rising above the trees. At first it moved slowly, rolling, forming, expanding, blooming like a column of whirling gray smoke; then it gathered headway and rolled onward through the forest. A gray, gloomy curtain, moving and rippling, split by the trees, seemed to be passing over us. It rose higher and higher, to split up in great globes, to roll apart, showing glimpses of blue sky.

Shafts of golden sunshine shot down from these rifts, dispelling the shadows and gloom, moving in paths of gold through the forest glade, gleaming with brilliantly colored fire from the snow-wreathed pines.

The cloud rolled away and the sun shone hot. The

trees began to drip. A mist of diamonds filled the
air, rainbows curved through every glade and feathered patches of snow floated down.

A great bank of snow, sliding from the pine over-
head almost buried the Navajo, to our infinite delight. We all sought the shelter of the tents, and
sleep again claimed us.

I awoke about five o'clock. The sun was low,
making crimson paths in the white aisles of the
forest. A cold wind promised a frosty morning.

"To-morrow will be the day for lions," exclaimed
Jones.

While we hugged the fire, Navvy brought up the
horses and gave them their oats. The hounds sought
their shelter and the lions lay hidden in their beds of
pine. The round red sun dropped out of sight beyond
the trees, a pink glow suffused all the ridges; blue
shadows gathered in the hollow, shaded purple and
stole upward. A brief twilight succeeded to a dark,
coldly starlit night.

Once again, when I had crawled into the warm
hole of my sleeping bag, was I hailed from the other
tent.

Emett called me twice, and as I answered, I heard
Jones remonstrating in a low voice.

"Shore, Jones has got 'em!" yelled Jim. "He
can't keep it a secret no longer."

"Hey, Jones," I cried, "do you remember laughing at me?"

"No, I don't," growled Jones.

"Listen to this: Haw-haw! haw! haw! ho-ho! ho-ho!
bueno! bueno!" and I wound up with a string of
"hi! hi! hi! hi! hi!"

The hounds rose up in a body and began to yelp.

"Lie down, pups," I called to them. "Nothing doing for you. It's only Jones has got 'em."

XII

When we trooped out of the pines next morning, the sun, rising gloriously bright, had already taken off the keen edge of the frosty air, presaging a warm day. The white ridges glistened; the bunches of sage scintillated, and the cedars, tipped in snow, resembled trees with brilliant blossoms.

We lost no time riding for the mouth of Left Canyon, into which Jim had trailed the three lions. On the way the snow, as we had expected, began to thin out, and it failed altogether under the cedars, though there was enough on the branches to give us a drenching.

Jim reined in on the verge of a narrow gorge, and informed us the cave was below. Jones looked the ground over and said Jim had better take the hounds down while the rest of us remained above to await developments.

Jim went down on foot, calling the hounds and holding them close. We listened eagerly for him to yell or the pack to open up, but we were disappointed. In less than half an hour Jim came climbing out, with the information that the lions had left the cave, probably the evening after he had chased them there.

"Well, then," said Jones, "let's split the pack, and hunt round the rims of these canyons. We can signal to each other if necessary."

So we arranged for Jim to take Ranger and the

pups across Left Canyon; Emett to try Middle Canyon, with Don and Moze, and we were to perform a like office in Right Canyon with Sounder and Jude. Emett rode back with us, leaving us where we crossed Middle Canyon.

Jones and I rimmed a mile of our canyon and worked out almost to the west end of the Bay, without finding so much as a single track, so we started to retrace our way. The sun was now hot; the snow all gone; the ground dry as if it had never been damp; and Jones grumbled that no success would attend our efforts this morning.

We reached the ragged mouth of Right Canyon, where it opened into the deep, wide Bay, and because we hoped to hear our companions across the canyon, we rode close to the rim. Sounder and Jude both began to bark on a cliff; however, as we could find no tracks in the dust we called them off. Sounder obeyed reluctantly, but Jude wanted to get down over the wall.

"They scent a lion," averred Jones. "Let's put them over the wall."

Once permitted to go, the hounds needed no assistance. They ran up and down the rim till they found a crack. Hardly had they gone out of sight when we heard them yelping. We rushed to the rim and looked over. The first step was short, a crumbled section of wall, and from it led down a long slope, dotted here and there with cedars. Both hounds were baying furiously.

I spied Jude with her paws up on a cedar, and above her hung a lion, so close that she could nearly reach him. Sounder was not yet in sight.

"There! There!" I cried, directing Jones' glance. "Are we not lucky?"

"I see. By George! Come, we'll go down. Leave everything that you don't absolutely need."

Spurs, chaps, gun, coat, hat, I left on the rim, taking only my camera and lasso. I had forgotten to bring my canteen. We descended a ladder of shaly cliff, the steps of which broke under our feet. The slope below us was easy, and soon we stood on a level with the lion. The cedar was small, and afforded no good place for him. Evidently he jumped from the slope to the tree, and had hung where he first alighted.

"Where's Sounder? Look for him. I hear him below. This lion won't stay treed long."

I, too, heard Sounder. The cedar tree obstructed my view, and I moved aside. A hundred feet farther down the hound bayed under a tall piñon. High in the branches I saw a great mass of yellow, and at first glance thought Sounder had treed old Sultan. How I yelled! Then a second glance showed two lions close together.

"Two more! two more! look! look!" I yelled to Jones.

"Hi! Hi! Hi!" he joined his robust yell to mine, and for a moment we made the canyon bellow. When we stopped for breath the echoes bayed at us from the opposite walls.

"Waa-hoo!" Emett's signal, faint, far away, soaring but unmistakable, floated down to us. Across the jutting capes separating the mouths of these canyons, high above them on the rim wall of the opposite side of the Bay, stood a giant white horse silhouetted against the white sky. They made a brave picture, one most welcome to us. We yelled in chorus: "Three lions treed! Three lions treed! come down—hurry!"

A crash of rolling stones made us wheel. Jude's lion had jumped. He ran straight down, drawing Sounder from his guard. Jude went tearing after them.

"I'll follow; you stay here. Keep them up there, if you can!" yelled Jones. Then in long strides he passed down out of sight among the trees and crags.

It had all happened so quickly that I could scarcely realize it. The yelping of the hounds, the clattering of stones, grew fainter, telling me Jude and Sounder, with Jones, were going to the bottom of the Bay.

Both lions snarling at me brought me to a keen appreciation of the facts in the case. Two full-grown lions to be kept treed without hounds, without a companion, without a gun.

"This is fine! This is funny!" I cried, and for a moment I wanted to run. But the same grim, deadly feeling that had taken me with Don around the narrow shelf now rose in me stronger and fiercer. I pronounced one savage malediction upon myself for leaving my gun. I could not go for it; I would have to make the best of my error, and in the wildness born of the moment I swore if the lions would stay treed for the hounds they would stay treed for me.

First I photographed them from different positions; then I took up my stand about on a level with them in an open place on the slope where they had me in plain sight. I might have been fifty feet from them. They showed no inclination to come down.

About this moment I heard hounds below, coming down from the left. I called and called, but they

passed on down the canyon bottom in the direction
Jones had taken.

Presently a chorus of bays, emphasized by Jones'
yell, told me his lion had treed again.

"Waa-hoo!" rolled down from above.

I saw Emett farther to the left from the point
where he had just appeared.

"Where—can—I—get—down?"

I surveyed the walls of the Bay. Cliff on cliff,
slide on slide, jumble, crag, and ruin, baffled my
gaze. But I finally picked out a path.

"Farther to the left," I yelled, and waited. He
passed on, Don at his heels.

"There," I yelled again, "stop there; let Don go
down with your lasso, and come yourself."

I watched him swing the hound down a wall, and
pull the slip noose free. Don slid to the edge of a
slope, trotted to the right and left of crags, threaded
the narrow places, and turned in the direction of the
baying hounds. He passed on the verge of precipices
that made me tremble for him; but sure-footed as a
goat, he went on safely down, to disappear far to my
right.

Then I saw Emett sliding, leg wrapped around his
lasso, down the first step of the rim. His lasso,
doubled so as to reach round a cedar above, was too
short to extend to the landing below. He dropped,
raising a cloud of dust, and starting the stones.
Pulling one end of his lasso up around the cedar he
gathered it in a coil on his arm and faced forward,
following Don's trail.

What strides he took! In the clear light, with that
wild red and yellow background, with the stones and
gravel roaring down, streaming over the walls like

waterfalls, he seemed a giant pursuing a foe. From time to time he sent up a yell of encouragement that wound down the canyon, to be answered by Jones and the baying hounds and then the strange echoes. At last he passed out of sight behind the crests of the trees; I heard him going down, down till the sounds came up faint and hollow.

I was left absolutely alone with my two lions and never did a hunter so delight in a situation. I sat there in the sun watching them. For a long time they were quiet, listening. But as the bays and yells below diminished in volume and occurrence and then ceased altogether, they became restless. It was then that I, remembering the lion I had held on top of the crag, began to bark like a hound. The lions became quiet once more.

I bayed them for an hour. My voice grew from hoarse to hoarser, and finally failed in my throat. The lions immediately grew restless again. The lower one hissed, spat and growled at me, and made many attempts to start down, each one of which I frustrated by throwing stones under the tree. At length he made one more determined effort, turned head downward, and stepped from branch to branch.

I dashed down the incline with a stone in one hand and a long club in the other. Instinctively I knew I must hurt him—make him fear me. If he got far enough down to jump, he would either escape or have me helpless. I aimed deliberately at him, and hit him square in the ribs. He exploded in a spit-roar that raised my hair. Directly under him I wielded my club, pounded on the tree, thrashed at the branches and, like the crazy fool that I was, yelled at him:

"Go back! Go back! Don't you dare come down! I'd break your old head for you!"

Foolish or not, this means effectually stopped the descent. He climbed to his first perch. It was then, realizing what I had done, that I would certainly have made tracks from under the piñon, if I had not heard the faint yelp of a hound.

I listened. It came again, faint but clearer. I looked up at my lions. They too heard, for they were very still. I saw how strained they held their heads. I backed a little way up the slope. Then the faint yelp floated up again in the silence. Such dead, strange silence, that seemed never to have been broken! I saw the lions quiver, and if I ever heard anything in my life I heard their hearts thump. The yelp wafted up again, closer this time. I recognized it; it belonged to Don. The great hound on the back trail of the other lion was coming to my rescue.

"It's Don! It's Don! It's Don!" I cried, shaking my club at the lions. "It's all up with you now!" What feelings stirred me then! Pity for those lions dominated me. Big, tawny, cruel fellows as they were, they shivered with fright. Their sides trembled. But pity did not hold me long; Don's yelp, now getting clear and sharp, brought back the rush of savage, grim sensations.

A full-toned bay attracted my attention from the lions to the downward slope. I saw a yellow form moving under the trees and climbing fast. It was Don.

"Hi! Hi! old boy!" I yelled.

Then it seemed he moved up like a shot and stood all his long length, forepaws against the piñon, his deep bay ringing defiance to the lions.

It was a great relief, not to say a probable necessity, for me to sit down just then.

"Now come down," I said to my lions; "you can't catch that hound, and you can't get away from him."

Moments passed. I was just on the point of deciding to go down to hurry up my comrades, when I heard the other hounds coming. Yelp on yelp, bay on bay, made welcome music to my ears. Then a black and yellow, swiftly flying string of hounds bore into sight down the slope, streaked up and circled the piñon.

Jones, who at last showed his tall stooping form on the steep ascent, seemed as long in coming as the hounds had been swift.

"Did you get the lion? Where's Emett?" I asked in breathless eagerness.

"Lion tied—all fast," replied the panting Jones. "Left Emett—to guard—him."

"What are we to do now?"

"Wait—till I get my breath. Think out—a plan. We can't get both lions—out of one tree."

"All right," I replied, after a moment's thought. "I'll tie Sounder and Moze. You go up the tree. That first lion will jump, sure; he's almost ready now. Don and the other hounds will tree him again pretty soon. If he runs up the canyon, well and good. Then, if you can get the lasso on the other, I'll yell for Emett to come up to help you, and I'll follow Don."

Jones began the ascent of the piñon. The branches were not too close, affording him easy climbing. Before we looked for even a move on the part of the lions, the lower one began stepping down. I yelled a warning, but Jones did not have time to take advantage of it. He had half turned, meaning to swing out and drop, when the lion planted both forepaws upon his back. Jones went sprawling down with the lion almost on him.

Don had his teeth in the lion before he touched the ground, and when he did strike the rest of the hounds were on him. A cloud of dust rolled down the slope. The lion broke loose and with great, springy bounds ran up the canyon, Don and his followers hot-footing it after him.

Moze and Sounder broke the dead sapling to which I had tied them, and dragging it behind them, endeavored in frenzied action to join the chase. I drew them back, loosening the rope, so in case the other lion jumped I could free them quickly.

Jones calmly gathered himself up, rearranged his lasso, took his long stick, and proceeded to mount the piñon again. I waited till I saw him slip the noose over the lion's head, then I ran down the slope to yell for Emett. He answered at once. I told him to hurry to Jones' assistance. With that I headed up the canyon.

I hung close to the broad trail left by the lion and his pursuers. I passed perilously near the brink of precipices, but fear of them was not in me that day. I passed out of the Bay into the mouth of Left Canyon, and began to climb. The baying of the hounds directed me. In the box of yellow walls the chorus seemed to come from a hundred dogs.

When I found them, close to a low cliff, baying the lion in a thick, dark piñon, Ranger leaped into my arms and next Don stood up against me with his paws on my shoulders. These were strange actions, and though I marked it at the moment, I had ceased to wonder at our hounds. I took one picture as the lion sat in the dark shade, and then climbed to the low cliff and sat down. I called Don to me and held him. In case our quarry leaped upon the cliff I wanted a hound to put quickly on his trail.

Another hour passed. It must have been a dark hour for the lion—he looked as if it were—and one of impatience for the baying hounds, but for me it was a full hour. Alone with the hounds and a lion, far from the walks of men, walled in by the wild-colored cliffs, with the dry, sweet smell of cedar and piñon, I asked no more.

Sounder and Moze, vociferously venting their arrival, were forerunners to Jones. I saw his gray locks waving in the breeze, and yelled for him to take his time. As he reached me the lion jumped and ran up the canyon. This suited me, for I knew he would take to a tree soon and the farther up he went the less distance we would have to pack him. From the cliff I saw him run up a slope, pass a big cedar, cunningly turn on his trail, and then climb into the tree and hide in its thickest part. Don passed him, got off the trail, and ran at fault. The others, so used to his leadership, were also baffled. But Jude, crippled and slow, brought up the rear, and she did not go a yard beyond where the lion turned. She opened up her deep call under the cedar, and in a moment the howling pack were around her.

Jones and I toiled laboriously upward. He had brought my lasso, and he handed it to me with the significant remark that I would soon have need of it.

The cedar was bushy and overhung a yellow, bare slope that made Jones shake his head. He climbed the tree, lassoed the spitting lion and then leaped down to my side. By united and determined efforts we pulled the lion off the limb and let him down. The hounds began to leap at him. We both roared in a rage at them but to no use.

"Hold him there!" shouted Jones, leaving me with the lasso while he sprang forward.

The weight of the animal dragged me forward and, had I not taken a half hitch round a dead snag, would have lifted me off my feet or pulled the lasso from my hands. As it was, the choking lion, now within reach of the furious, leaping hounds, swung to and fro before my face. He could not see me, but his frantic lunges narrowly missed me.

If never before, Jones then showed his genius. Don had hold of the lion's flank, and Jones, grabbing the hound by the hind legs, threw him down the slope. Don fell and rolled a hundred feet before he caught himself. Then Jones threw old Moze rolling, and Ranger, and all except faithful Jude. Before they could get back he roped the lion again and made fast to a tree. Then he yelled for me to let go. The lion fell. Jones grabbed the lasso, at the same time calling for me to stop the hounds. As they came bounding up the steep slope, I had to club the noble fellows into submission.

Before the lion recovered wholly from his severe choking, we had his paws bound fast. Then he could only heave his tawny sides, glare and spit at us.

"Now what?" asked Jones. "Emett is watching the second lion, which we fastened by chain and lasso to a swinging branch. I'm all in. My heart won't stand any more climb."

"You go to camp for the pack horses," I said

briefly. "Bring them all, and all the packs, and Navvy, too. I'll help Emett tie up the second lion, and then we'll pack them both up here to this one. You take the hounds with you."

"Can you tie up that lion?" asked Jones. "Mind you, he's loose except for a collar and chain. His claws haven't been clipped. Besides, it'll be an awful job to pack those two lions up here."

"We can try," I said. "You hustle to camp. Your horse is right up back of here, across the point, if I don't mistake my bearings."

Jones, admonishing me again, called the hounds and wearily climbed the slope. I waited until he was out of hearing; then began to retrace my trail down into the canyon. I made the descent in quick time, to find Emett standing guard over the lion. The beast had been tied to an overhanging branch that swung violently with every move he made.

"When I got here," said Emett, "he was hanging over the side of that rock, almost choked to death. I drove him into this corner between the rocks and the tree, where he has been comparatively quiet. Now, what's up? Where is Jones? Did you get the third lion?"

I related what had occurred, and then said we were to tie this lion and pack him with the other one up the canyon, to meet Jones and the horses.

"All right," replied Emett, with a grim laugh. "We'd better get at it. Now I'm some worried about the lion we left below. He ought to be brought up, but we both can't go. This lion here will kill himself."

"What will the other one weigh?"

"All of one hundred and fifty pounds."

"You can't pack him alone."

"I'll try, and I reckon that's the best plan. Watch this fellow and keep him in the corner."

Emett left me then, and I began a third long vigil beside a lion. The rest was more than welcome. An hour and a half passed before I heard the sliding of stones below, which told me that Emett was coming. He appeared on the slope almost bent double, carrying the lion, head downward, before him. He could climb only a few steps without lowering his burden and resting.

I ran down to meet him. We secured a stout pole, and slipping this between the lion's paws, below where they were tied, we managed to carry him fairly well, and after several rests, got him up alongside the other.

"Now to tie that rascal!" exclaimed Emett. "Jones said he was the meanest one he'd tackled, and I believe it. We'll cut a piece off of each lasso, and unravel them so as to get strings. I wish Jones hadn't tied the lasso to that swinging branch."

"I'll go and untie it." Acting on this suggestion I climbed the tree and started out on the branch. The lion growled fiercely.

"I'm afraid you'd better stop," warned Emett. "That branch is bending, and the lion can reach you."

But despite this I slipped out a couple of yards farther, and had almost gotten to the knotted lasso, when the branch swayed and bent alarmingly. The lion sprang from his corner and crouched under me snarling and spitting, with every indication of leaping.

"Jump! Jump! Jump!" shouted Emett hoarsely.

I dared not, for I could not jump far enough to get out of the lion's reach. I raised my legs and began to slide myself back up the branch. The lion leaped, missing me, but scattering the dead twigs. Then the beast, beside himself with fury, half leaped, half stood up, and reached for me. I looked down into his blazing eyes, and open mouth and saw his white fangs.

Everything grew blurred before my eyes. I desperately fought for control over mind and muscle. I heard hoarse roars from Emett. Then I felt a hot, burning pain in my wrist, which stung all my faculties into keen life again.

I saw the lion's beaked claws fastened in my leather wrist-band. At the same instant Emett dashed under the branch, and grasped the lion's tail. One powerful lunge of his broad shoulders tore the lion loose and flung him down the slope to the full extent of his lasso. Quick as thought I jumped down, and just in time to prevent Emett from attacking the lion with the heavy pole we had used.

"I'll kill him! I'll kill him!" roared Emett.

"No you won't," I replied, quietly, for my pain had served to soothe my excitement as well as to make me more determined. "We'll tie up the darned tiger, if he cuts us all to pieces. You know how Jones will give us the laugh if we fail. Here, bind up my wrist."

Mention of Jones' probable ridicule and sight of my injury cooled Emett.

"It's a nasty scratch," he said, binding my handkerchief round it. "The leather saved your hand from being torn off. He's an ugly brute, but you're right, we'll tie him. Now, let's each take a lasso and worry him till we get hold of a paw. Then we can stretch him out."

Jones did a fiendish thing when he tied that lion to the swinging branch. It was almost worse than having him entirely free. He had a circle almost twenty feet in diameter in which he could run and leap at will. It seemed he was in the air all the time. First at Emett, than at me he sprang, mouth agape, eyes wild, claws spread. We whipped him with our nooses, but not one would hold. He always tore it off before we could draw it tight. I secured a precarious hold on one hind paw and straightened my lasso.

"That's far enough," cried Emett. "Now hold him tight; don't lift him off the ground."

I had backed up the slope. Emett faced the lion, noose ready, waiting for a favorable chance to rope a front paw. The lion crouched low and tense, only his long tail lashing back and forth across my lasso. Emett threw the loop in front of the spread paws, now half sunk into the dust.

"Ease up; ease up," said he. "I'll tease him to jump into the noose."

I let my rope sag. Emett poked a stick into the lion's face. All at once I saw the slack in the lasso which was tied to the lion's chain. Before I could yell to warn my comrade the beast leaped. My rope burned as it tore through my hands. The lion sailed into the air, his paws wide-spread like wings, and one of them struck Emett on the head and rolled him on the slope. I jerked back on my rope only to find it had slipped its hold.

"He slugged me one," remarked Emett, calmly rising and picking up his hat. "Did he break the skin?"

"No, but he tore your hat band off," I replied. "Let's keep at him."

For a few moments or an hour—no one will ever know how long—we ran round him, raising the dust, scattering the stones, breaking the branches, dodging his onslaughts. He leaped at us to the full length of his tether, sailing right into our faces, a fierce, uncowed, tigerish beast. If it had not been for the collar and swivel he would have choked himself a hundred times. Quick as a cat, supple, powerful, tireless, he kept on the go, whirling, bounding, leaping, rolling, till it seemed we would never catch him.

"If anything breaks, he'll get one of us," cried Emett. "I felt his breath that time."

"Lord! How I wish we had some of those fellows here who say lions are rank cowards!" I exclaimed.

In one of his sweeping side swings the lion struck the rock and hung there on its flat surface with his tail hanging over.

"Attract his attention," shouted Emett, "but don't get too close. Don't make him jump."

While I slowly manoeuvered in front of the lion, Emett slipped behind the rock, lunged for the long tail and got a good hold of it. Then with a whoop he ran around the rock, carrying the kicking, squalling lion clear of the ground.

"Now's your chance," he yelled. "Rope a hind foot! I can hold him."

In a second I had a noose fast on both hind paws, and then passed my rope to Emett. While he held the lion I again climbed the tree, untied the knot that had caused so much trouble, and very shortly we had our obstinate captive stretched out between two trees. After that we took a much needed breathing spell.

"Not very scientific," growled Emett, by way of

apologizing for our crude work, "but we had to get him some way."

"Emett, do you know I believe Jones put up a job on us?" I said.

"Well, maybe he did. We had the job all right. But we'll make short work of him now."

He certainly went at it in a way that alarmed me and would have electrified Jones. While I held the chain Emett muzzled the lion with a stick and a strand of lasso. His big blacksmith's hands held, twisted and tied with remorseless strength.

"Now for the hardest part of it," said he, "packing him up."

We toiled and drudged upward, resting every few yards, wet with sweat, boiling with heat, parching for water. We slipped and fell, got up to slip and fall again. The dust choked us. We senselessly risked our lives on the brinks of precipices. We had no thought save to get the lion up. One hour of unremitting labor saw our task finished, so far. Then we wearily went down for the other.

"This one is the heaviest," gloomily said Emett.

We had to climb partly sidewise with the pole in the hollow of our elbows. The lion dragged head downward, catching in the brush and on the stones. Our rests became more frequent. Emett, who had the downward end of the pole, and therefore thrice the weight, whistled when he drew breath. Half the time I saw red mist before my eyes. How I hated the sliding stones!

"Wait," panted Emett once. "You're—younger—than me—wait!"

For that Mormon giant—used all his days to strenuous toil, peril and privation—to ask me to wait for him, was a compliment which I valued more than any I had ever received.

At last we dropped our burden in the shade of a cedar where the other lions lay, and we stretched ourselves. A long, sweet rest came abruptly to end with Emett's next words.

"The lions are choking! They're dying of thirst! We must have water!"

One glance at the poor, gasping, frothing beasts, proved to me the nature of our extremity.

"Water in this desert! Where will we find it? Oh! why, did I forget my canteen!"

After all our hopes, our efforts, our tragedies, and finally our wonderful good fortune, to lose these beautiful lions for lack of a little water was sickening, maddening.

"Think quick!" cried Emett. "I'm no good; I'm all in. But you must find water. It snowed yesterday. There's water somewhere."

Into my mind flashed a picture of the many little pockets beaten by rains into the shelves and promontories of the canyon rim. With the thought I was on the jump. I ran; I climbed; I seemed to have wings; I reached the rim, and hurried along it with eager gaze. I swung down on a cedar branch to a projecting point of rock. Small depressions were everywhere still damp, but the water had evaporated. But I would not give up. I jumped from rock to rock, and climbed over scaly ledges, and set tons of yellow shale into motion. And I found on a ragged promontory many little, round holes, some a foot deep, all full of clear water. Using my handkerchief as a sponge I filled my cap.

Then began my journey down. I carried the cap

with both hands and balanced myself like a tight-rope performer. I zigzaged the slopes; slipped over stones; leaped fissures and traversed yellow slides. I safely descended places that in an ordinary moment would have presented insurmountable obstacles, and burst down upon Emett with an Indian yell of triumph.

"Good!" ejaculated he. If I had not known it already, the way his face changed would have told me of his love for animals. He grasped a lion by the ears and held his head up. I saturated my handkerchief and squeezed the water into his mouth. He wheezed, coughed, choked, but to our joy he swallowed. He had to swallow. One after the other we served them so, seeing with unmistakable relief the sure signs of recovery. Their eyes cleared and brightened; the dry coughing that distressed us so ceased; the froth came no more. The savage fellow that had fought us to a standstill, and for which we had named him Spitfire, raised his head, the gold in his beautiful eyes darkened to fire and he growled his return to life and defiance.

Emett and I sank back in unutterable relief.

"Waa-hoo!" Jones' yell came, breaking the warm quiet of the slope. Our comrade appeared riding down. The voice of the Indian, calling to Marc, mingled with the ringing of iron-shod hoofs on the stones.

Jones surveyed the small level spot in the shade of the cedars. He gazed from the lions to us, his stern face relaxed, and his dry laugh cracked.

"Doggone me, if you didn't do it!"

XIII

A strange procession soon emerged from Left Canyon and stranger to us than the lion heads bobbing out of the alfagoes was the sight of Navvy riding in front of the lions. I kept well in the rear, for if anything happened, which I calculated was more than likely, I wanted to see it. Before we had reached the outskirts of pines, I observed that the piece of lasso around Spitfire's nose had worked loose.

Just as I was about to make this known to Jones, the lion opened a corner of his mouth and fastened his teeth in the Navajo's overalls. He did not catch the flesh, for when Navvy turned around he wore only an expression of curiosity. But when he saw Spitfire chewing him he uttered a shrill scream and fell sidewise off his horse.

Then two difficulties presented themselves to us, to catch the frightened horse and persuade the Indian he had not been bitten. We failed in the latter. Navvy gave us and the lions a wide berth, and walked to camp.

Jim was waiting for us, and said he had chased a lion south along the rim till the hounds got away from him.

Spitfire, having already been chained, was the first lion we endeavored to introduce to our family of captives. He raised such a fearful row that we had to remove him some distance from the others.

"We have two dog chains," said Jones, "but not a collar or a swivel in camp. We can't chain the lions without swivels. They'd choke themselves in two minutes."

Once more, for the hundredth time, Emett came to

our rescue with his inventive and mechanical skill. He took the largest pair of hobbles we had, and with an axe, a knife and Jones' wire nippers, fashioned two collars with swivels that for strength and serviceableness improved somewhat on those we had bought.

Darkness was enveloping the forest when we finished supper. I fell into my bed and, despite the throbbing and burning of my wrist, soon lapsed into slumber. And I crawled out next morning late for breakfast, stiff, worn out, crippled, but happy. Six lions roaring a concert for me was quite conducive to contentment.

Emett interestingly engaged himself on a new pair of trousers, which he had contrived to produce from two of our empty meal-bags. The lower half of his overalls had gone to decorate the cedar spikes and brush, and these new bag-leg trousers, while somewhat remarkable for design, answered the purpose well enough. Jones' coat was somewhere along the canyon rim, his shoes were full of holes, his shirt in strips, and his trousers in rags. Jim looked like a scarecrow. My clothes, being of heavy waterproofed duck, had stood the hard usage in a manner to bring forth the unanimous admiration of my companions.

"Well, fellows," said Jones, "there's six lions, and that's more than we can pack out of here. Have you had enough hunting? I have."

"And I," rejoined Emett.

"Shore you can bet I have," drawled Jim.

"One more day, boys, and then I've done," said I. "Only one more day!"

Signs of relief on the faces of my good comrades

showed how they took this evidence of my satisfied ambition.

I spent all the afternoon with the lions, photographing them, listening to them spit and growl, watching them fight their chains, and roll up like balls of fire. From different parts of the forest I tried to creep unsuspected upon them; but always when I peeped out from behind a tree or log, every pair of ears would be erect, every pair of eyes gleaming and suspicious.

Spitfire afforded more amusement than all the others. He had indeed the temper of a king; he had been born for sovereignty, not slavery. To intimidate me he tried every manner of expression and utterance, and failing, he always ended with a spring in the air to the length of his chain. This means was always effective. I simply could not stand still when he leaped; and in turn I tried every artifice I could think of to make him back away from me, to take refuge behind his tree. I ran at him with a club as if I were going to kill him. He waited, crouching. Finally, in dire extremity, I bethought me of a red flannel hood that Emett had given me, saying I might use it on cold nights. This was indeed a weird, flaming headgear, falling like a cloak down over the shoulders. I put it on, and, camera in hand, started to crawl on all fours toward Spitfire.

I needed no one to tell me that this proceeding was entirely beyond his comprehension. In his astonishment he forgot to spit and growl, and he backed behind the little pine, from which he regarded me with growing perplexity. Then, having revenged myself on him, and getting a picture, I left him in peace.

XIV

I awoke before dawn, and lay watching the dark shadows change into gray, and gray into light. The Navajo chanted solemnly and low his morning song. I got up with the keen eagerness of the hunter who faces the last day of his hunt.

I warmed my frozen fingers at the fire. A hot breakfast smoked on the red coals. We ate while Navvy fed and saddled the horses.

"Shore, they'll be somethin' doin' to-day," said Jim, fatalistically.

"We haven't crippled a horse yet," put in Emett hopefully. Don led the pack and us down the ridge, out of the pines into the sage. The sun, a red ball, glared out of the eastern mist, shedding a dull glow on the ramparts of the far canyon walls. A herd of white-tailed deer scattered before the hounds. Blue grouse whirred from under our horses' feet.

"Spread out," ordered Jones, and though he meant the hounds, we all followed his suggestion, as the wisest course.

Ranger began to work up the sage ridge to the right. Jones, Emett and I followed, while Jim rode away to the left. Gradually the space widened, and as we neared the cedars, a sharply defined, deep canyon separated us.

We heard Don open up, then Sounder. Ranger left the trail he was trying to work out in the thick sage, and bounded in the direction of the rest of the pack. We reined in to listen.

First Don, then Sounder, then Jude, then one of the pups bayed eagerly, telling us they were hunting hard. Suddenly the bays blended in one savage sound.

"Hi! Hi! Hi!" cracked the cool, thin air. We saw Jim wave his hand from the far side of the canyon, spur his horse into action, and disappear into the cedars.

"Stick close together," yelled Jones, as we launched forward. We made the mistake of not going back to cross the canyon, for the hounds soon went up the opposite side. As we rode on and on, the sounds of the chase lessened, and finally ceased. To our great chagrin we found it necessary to retrace our steps, and when we did get over the deep gully, so much time had elapsed that we despaired of coming up with Jim. Emett led, keeping close on Jim's trail, which showed plain in the dust, and we followed.

Up and down ravines, over ridges, through sage flats and cedar forests, to and fro, around and around, we trailed Jim and the hounds. From time to time one of us let let out a long yell.

"I see a big lion track," called Jones once, and that stirred us on faster. Fully an hour passed before Jones halted us, saying we had best try a signal. I dismounted, while Emett rolled his great voice through the cedars.

A long silence ensued. From the depths of the forest Jim's answer struck faintly on my ear. With a word to my companions I leaped on my mustang and led the way. I rode as far as I could mark a straight line with my eye, then stopped to wait for another cry. In this way, slowly but surely we closed in on Jim.

We found him on the verge of the Bay, in the small glade where I had left my horse the day I followed Don alone down the canyon. Jim was engaged in binding up the leg of his horse. The baying of the hounds floated up over the rim.

"What's up?" queried Jones.

"Old Sultan. That's what," replied Jim. "We run plumb into him. We've had him in five trees. It ain't been long since he was in that cedar there. When he jumped the yellow pup was in the way an' got killed. My horse just managed to jump clear of the big lion, an' as it was, nearly broke his leg."

Emett examined the leg and pronounced it badly strained, and advised Jim to lead the horse back to camp. Jones and I stood a moment over the remains of the yellow pup, and presently Emett joined us.

"He was the most playful one of the pack," said Emett, and then he placed the limp, bloody body in a crack, and laid several slabs of stone over it.

"Hurry after the other hounds," said Jim. "That lion will kill them one by one. An' look out for him!"

If we needed an incentive, the danger threatening the hounds furnished one; but I calculated the death of the pup was enough. Emett had a flare in his eye, Jones looked darker and more grim than ever, and I had sensations that boded ill to old Sultan.

"Fellows," I said, "I've been down this place, and I know where the old brute has gone; so come on."

I laid aside my coat, chaps and rifle, feeling that the business ahead was stern and difficult. Then I faced the canyon. Down slopes, among rocks, under piñons, around yellow walls, along slides, the two big men followed me with heavy steps. We reached the white stream-bed, and sliding, slipping, jumping, always down and down, we came at last within sound of the hounds. We found them baying wildly under a piñon on the brink of the deep cove.

Then, at once, we all saw old Sultan close at hand. He was of immense size; his color was almost gray; his head huge, his paws heavy and round. He did not spit, nor snarl, nor growl; he did not look at the hounds, but kept his half-shut eyes upon us.

We had no time to make a move before he left his perch and hit the ground with a thud. He walked by the baying hounds, looked over the brink of the cove, and without an instant of hesitation, leaped down. The rattling crash of sliding stones came up with a cloud of dust. Then we saw him leisurely picking his way among the rough stones.

Exclamations from the three of us attested to what we thought of that leap.

"Look the place over," called Jones. "I think we've got him."

The cove was a hole hollowed out by running water. At its head, where the perpendicular wall curved, the height was not less than forty feet. The walls became higher as the cove deepened toward the canyon. It had a length of perhaps a hundred yards, and a width of perhaps half as many. The floor was mass on mass of splintered rock.

"Let the hounds down on a lasso," said Jones.

Easier said than done! Sounder, Ranger, Jude refused. Old Moze grumbled and broke away. But Don, stern and savage, allowed Jones to tie him in a slip noose.

"It's a shame to send that grand hound to his death," protested Emett.

"We'll all go down," declared Jones.

"We can't. One will have to stay up here to help the other two out," replied Emett.

"You're the strongest; you stay up," said Jones. "Better work along the wall and see if you can locate the lion."

We let Don down into the hole. He kicked himself loose before reaching the bottom and then, yelping, he went out of sight among the boulders. Moze, as if ashamed, came whining to us. We slipped a noose around him and lowered him, kicking and barking, to the rocky floor. Jones made the lasso fast to a cedar root, and I slid down, like a flash, burning my hands. Jones swung himself over, wrapped his leg around the rope, and came down, to hit the ground with a thump. Then, lassos in hands, we began clambering over the broken fragments.

For a few moments we were lost to sights and sounds away from our immediate vicinity. The bottom of the cove afforded hard going. Dead piñons and cedars blocked our way; the great, jagged stones offered no passage. We crawled, climbed, and jumped from piece to piece.

A yell from Emett halted us. We saw him above, on the extreme point of wall. Waving his arms, he yelled unintelligible commands to us. The fierce baying of Don and Moze added to our desperate energy.

The last jumble of splintered rock cleared, we faced a terrible and wonderful scene.

"Look! Look!" I gasped to Jones.

A wide, bare strip of stone lay a few yards beneath us; and in the center of this last step sat the great lion on his haunches with his long tail lashing out over the precipice. Back to the canyon, he confronted the furious hounds; his demeanor had changed to one of savage apprehension.

When Jones and I appeared, old Sultan abruptly turned his back to the hounds and looked down into the canyon. He walked the whole length of the bare rock with his head stretched over. He was looking for a niche or a step whereby he might again elude his foes.

Faster lashed his tail; farther and farther stretched his neck. He stopped, and with head bent so far over the abyss that it seemed he must fall, he looked and looked.

How grandly he fitted the savage sublimity of that place! The tremendous purple canyon depths lay beneath him. He stood on the last step of his mighty throne. The great downward slopes had failed him. Majestically and slowly he turned from the deep that offered no hope.

As he turned, Jones cast the noose of his lasso perfectly round the burly neck. Sultan roared and worked his jaws, but he did not leap. Jones must have expected such a move, for he fastened his rope to a spur of rock. Standing there, revolver gripped, hearing the baying hounds, the roaring lion, and Jones' yells mingled with Emett's, I had no idea what to do. I was in a trance of sensations.

Old Sultan ran rather than leaped at us. Jones evaded the rush by falling behind a stone, but still did not get out of danger. Don flew at the lion's neck and Moze buried his teeth in a flank. Then the three rolled on the rock dangerously near the verge.

Bellowing, Jones grasped the lasso and pulled. Still holding my revolver, I leaped to his assistance, and together we pulled and jerked. Don got away from the lion with remarkable quickness. But Moze, slow and dogged, could not elude the outstretched paws, which fastened in his side and leg. We pulled so hard we slowly raised the lion. Moze, never whimpering, clawed and scratched at the rock in his efforts to escape. The lion's red tongue protruded from his dripping jaws. We heard the rend of hide as our efforts, combined with those of Moze, loosed him from the great yellow claws.

The lion, whirling and wrestling, rolled over the precipice. When the rope straightened with a twang, had it not been fastened to the rock, Jones and I would have jerked over the wall. The shock threw us to our knees.

For a moment we did not realize the situation. Emett's yells awakened us.

"Pull! Pull! Pull!" roared he.

Then, knowing that old Sultan would hang himself in a few moments, we attempted to lift him. Jones pulled till his back cracked; I pulled till I saw red before my eyes. Again and again we tried. We could lift him only a few feet. Soon exhausted, we had to desist altogether. How Emett roared and raged from his vantage-point above! He could see the lion in death throes.

Suddenly he quieted down with the words: "All over; all over!" Then he sat still, looking into space. Jones sat mopping his brow. And I, all my hot resentment vanished, lay on the rock, with eyes on the distant mesas.

Presently Jones leaned over the verge with my lasso.

"There," he said, "I've roped one of his hind

legs. Now we'll pull him up a little, then we'll fasten this rope, and pull on the other.''

So, foot by foot, we worked the heavy lion up over the wall. He must have been dead, though his sides heaved. Don sniffed at him in disdain. Moze, dusty and bloody, with a large strip of hide hanging from his flank, came up growling low and deep, and gave the lion a last vengeful bite.

''We've been fools,'' observed Jones, meditatively. ''The excitement of the game made us lose our wits. I'll never rope another lion.''

I said nothing. While Moze licked his bloody leg and Don lay with his fine head on my knees, Jones began to skin old Sultan. Once more the strange, infinite silence enfolded the canyon. The far-off golden walls glistened in the sun; farther down, the purple clefts smoked. The many-hued peaks and mesas, aloof from each other, rose out of the depths. It was a grand and gloomy scene of ruin where every glistening descent of rock was but a page of earth's history.

It brought to my mind a faint appreciation of what time really meant; it spoke of an age of former men; it showed me the lonesome crags of eagles, and the cliff lairs of lions; and it taught mutely, eloquently, a lesson of life—that men are still savage, still driven by a spirit to roam, to hunt, and to slay.